George Gordon Byron

The Gallery of Byron Beauties

Ideal pictures of the principal female characters in Lord Byron's poems

George Gordon Byron

The Gallery of Byron Beauties
Ideal pictures of the principal female characters in Lord Byron's poems

ISBN/EAN: 9783337052256

Printed in Europe, USA, Canada, Australia, Japan

Cover: Foto ©Thomas Meinert / pixelio.de

More available books at **www.hansebooks.com**

THE GALLERY

OF

BYRON BEAUTIES:

Ideal Pictures

OF

THE PRINCIPAL FEMALE CHARACTERS

IN

LORD BYRON'S POEMS.

FROM ORIGINAL PAINTINGS BY EMINENT ARTISTS.

New York:
D. APPLETON AND COMPANY,
443 AND 445 BROADWAY.
MDCCCLX.

CONTENTS.

			PAGE
1.	CAROLINE,	MINOR POEMS,	7
2.	LESBIA,	MINOR POEMS,	11
3.	MARION,	MINOR POEMS,	13
4.	MORA,	MINOR POEMS,	17
5.	THE MAID OF ATHENS,	MINOR POEMS,	21
6.	THE MAID OF SARAGOZA,	CHILDE HAROLD,	23
7.	INEZ,	CHILDE HAROLD,	25
8.	FLORENCE,	CHILDE HAROLD,	29
9.	THE LIGHT OF THE HAREM,	CHILDE HAROLD,	35
10.	JULIA,	CHILDE HAROLD,	37
11.	THE YOUNG HAIDÉE,	MINOR POEMS,	39
12.	GENEVRA,	MINOR POEMS,	41
13.	LEILA,	GIAOUR,	43
14.	ZULEIKA,	BRIDE OF ABYDOS,	49
15.	MEDORA,	CORSAIR,	55
16.	GULNARE,	CORSAIR,	61
17.	KALED,	LARA,	67
18.	JEPHTHA'S DAUGHTER,	HEBREW MELODIES,	71
19.	PARISINA,	PARISINA,	73
20.	ASTARTE,	MANFRED,	77
21.	LEONORA,	LAMENT OF TASSO,	81
22.	LAURA,	BEPPO,	83

			PAGE
23. THERESA,	. MAZEPPA, . .	85
24. BEATRICE,	PROPHECY OF DANTE,	89
25. ANGIOLINA, . . .	. MARINO FALIERO,	91
26. ANAH AND AHOLIBAMAH, .	HEAVEN AND EARTH,	115
27. MYRRHA, .	. SARDANAPALUS, . .	. 123
28. OLIMPIA, .	DEFORMED TRANSFORMED, .	137
29. ADAH, . .	. CAIN, ...	. 143
30. DONNA INEZ,	DON JUAN,	151
31. DONNA JULIA,	. DON JUAN,	. 155
32. HAIDÉE,	DON JUAN,	159
33. ZOE, .	. DON JUAN, .	. 165
34. GULBEYAZ,	DON JUAN,	167
35. KATINKA,	. DON JUAN, .	. 171
36. DUDÙ, . . .	DON JUAN,	173
37. LADY PINCHBECK,	. DON JUAN, .	. 175
38. AURORA RABY, . . .	DON JUAN,	177
39. THE DUCHESS OF FITZ-FULKE,	. DON JUAN, .	. 181

LIST OF PLATES.

			PAGE
1. CAROLINE,		F. CORBAUX,	7
2. LESBIA,		F. CORBAUX,	11
3. MARION,		F. CORBAUX,	13
4. MORA,		F. CORBAUX,	17
5. THE MAID OF ATHENS,		MEADOWS,	21
6. THE MAID OF SARAGOZA,		J. F. LEWIS,	23
7. INEZ,		F. STONE,	25
8. FLORENCE,		F. STONE,	29
9. THE LIGHT OF THE HAREM,		E. WOOD,	35
10. JULIA,		W. BOXALL,	37
11. THE YOUNG HAIDÉE,		G. BROWNE,	39
12. GENEVRA,		F. CORBAUX,	41
13. LEILA,		F. CORBAUX,	43
14. ZULEIKA,		J. W. WRIGHT,	49
15. MEDORA,		MEADOWS,	55
16. GULNARE,		F. CORBAUX,	61
17. KALED,		D. M'CLISE,	67
18. JEPHTHA'S DAUGHTER,		J. F. LEWIS,	71
19. PARISINA,		F. STONE,	73
20. ASTARTE,		H. CORBOULD,	77
21. LEONORA,		F. STONE,	81
22. LAURA,		W. BOXALL,	83

			PAGE
23. THERESA,	E. WOOD,		85
24. BEATRICE,	J. W. WRIGHT,		89
25. ANGIOLINA,	F. STONE,		91
26. ANAH AND AHOLIBAMAH,	F. STONE,		115
27. MYRRHA,	F. STONE,		123
28. OLIMPIA,	F. CORBAUX,		137
29. ADAH,	E. WOOD,		143
30. DONNA INEZ,	J. E. LEWIS,		151
31. DONNA JULIA,	J. E. LEWIS,		155
32. HAIDÉE,	A. E. CHALON, R. A.,		159
33. ZOE,	J. BOSTOCK,		165
34. GULBEYAZ,	MEADOWS,		167
35. KATINKA,	J. BOSTOCK,		171
36. DUDÙ,	MEADOWS,		173
37. LADY PINCHBECK,	W. BOXALL,		175
38. AURORA RABY,	E. WOOD,		177
39. THE DUCHESS OF FITZ-FULKE,	BOSTOCK,		181

THE BYRON GALLERY.

CAROLINE.

I.

Think'st thou I saw thy beauteous eyes,
   Suffused in tears, implore to stay;
And heard unmoved thy plenteous sighs,
   Which said far more than words can say?

Though keen the grief thy tears express'd,
   When love and hope lay both o'erthrown;
Yet still, my girl, this bleeding breast,
   Throbb'd with deep sorrow as thine own.

But when our cheeks with anguish glow'd,
   When thy sweet lips were join'd to mine,
The tears that from my eyelids flow'd
   Were lost in those which fell from thine.

Thou couldst not feel my burning cheek,
    Thy gushing tears had quenched its flame;
And as thy tongue essay'd to speak,
    In sighs alone it breathed my name.

And yet, my girl, we weep in vain,
    In vain our fate in sighs deplore;
Remembrance only can remain,—
    But that will make us weep the more.

Again, thou best beloved, adieu!
    Ah! if thou canst, o'ercome regret;
Nor let thy mind past joys review,—
    Our only hope is to forget!

II.

When I hear you express an affection so warm,
    Ne'er think, my beloved, that I do not believe;
For your lip would the soul of suspicion disarm,
    And your eye beams a ray which can never deceive.

Yet, still, this fond bosom regrets, while adoring,
    That love, like the leaf, must fall into the sear;
That age will come on, when remembrance, deploring,
    Contemplates the scenes of her youth with a tear;

That the time must arrive, when, no longer retaining
    Their auburn, those locks must wave thin to the breeze,
When a few silver hairs of those tresses remaining,
    Prove nature a prey to decay and disease.

'Tis this, my beloved, which spreads gloom o'er my features,
   Though I ne'er shall presume to arraign the decree,
Which God has proclaimed as the fate of his creatures,
   In the death which one day will deprive you of me.

Mistake not, sweet skeptic, the cause of emotion,
   No doubt can the mind of your lover invade;
He worships each look with such faithful devotion,
   A smile can enchant, or a tear can dissuade.

But as death, my beloved, soon or late shall o'ertake us,
   And our breasts, which alive with such sympathy glow,
Will sleep in the grave till the blast shall awake us,
   When calling the dead in earth's bosom laid low,—

Oh! then let us drain, while we may, draughts of pleasure,
   Which from passion like ours may unceasingly flow;
Let us pass round the cup of love's bliss in full measure,
   And quaff the contents as our nectar below.

III.

Oh! when shall the grave hide forever my sorrows?
   Oh! when shall my soul wing her flight from this clay?
The present is hell, and the coming to-morrow
   But brings, with new torture, the curse of to-day.

From my eye flows no tear, from my lips flow no curses,
   I blast not the fiends who have hurl'd me from bliss;
For poor is the soul which bewailing rehearses
   Its querulous grief, when in anguish like this.

Was my eye, 'stead of tears, with red fury flakes bright'ning,
    Would my lips breathe a flame which no stream could assuage,
On our foes should my glance launch in vengeance its lightning,
    With transport my tongue give a loose to its rage.

But now tears and curses, alike unavailing,
    Would add to the souls of our tyrants delight;
Could they view us our sad separation bewailing,
    Their merciless hearts would rejoice at the sight.

Yet still, though we bend with a feign'd resignation,
    Life beams not for us with one ray that can cheer;
Love and hope upon earth bring no more consolation;
    In the grave is our hope, for in life is our fear.

Oh! when, my adored, in the tomb will they place me,
    Since, in life, love and friendship forever are fled?
If again in the mansion of death I embrace thee,
    Perhaps they will leave unmolested the dead.

LESBIA.

Lesbia! since far from you I've ranged,
   Our souls with fond affection glow not;
You say 'tis I, not you, have changed,
   I'd tell you why,—but yet I know not.

Your polished brow no cares have cross'd;
   And, Lesbia! we are not much older,
Since, trembling, first my heart I lost,
   Or told my love, with hope grown bolder.

Sixteen was then our utmost age,
   Two years have lingering pass'd away, love!
And now new thoughts our minds engage,
   At least I feel disposed to stray, love!

'Tis I that am alone to blame,
   I that am guilty of love's treason;
Since your sweet breast is still the same,
   Caprice must be my only reason.

I do not, love! suspect your truth,
    With jealous doubt my bosom heaves not;
Warm was the passion of my youth,
    One trace of dark deceit it leaves not.

No, no, my flame was not pretended;
    For, oh! I loved you most sincerely;
And—though our dream at last is ended—
    My bosom still esteems you dearly.

No more we meet in yonder bowers;
    Absence has made me prone to roving;
But older, firmer hearts than ours
    Have found monotony in loving.

Your cheek's soft bloom is unimpair'd,
    New beauties still are daily bright'ning,
Your eye for conquest beams prepared,
    The forge of love's resistless lightning.

Arm'd thus, to make their bosoms bleed,
    Many will throng to sigh like me, love!
More constant they may prove, indeed;
    Fonder, alas! they ne'er can be, love!

MARION.

Marion! why that pensive brow?
What disgust to life hast thou?
Change that discontented air!
Frowns become not one so fair.
'Tis not love disturbs thy rest,
Love's a stranger to thy breast;
He in dimpling smiles appears,
Or mourns in sweetly timid tears,
Or bends the languid eyelid down;
But shuns the cold forbidding frown.
Then resume thy former fire,
Some will love, and all admire;
Wouldst thou wandering hearts beguile,
Smile at least, or seem to smile.
Eyes like thine were never meant
To hide their orbs in dark restraint;
Spite of all thou fain wouldst say,
Still in truant beams they play.
Thy lips—but here my modest Muse
Her impulse chaste must needs refuse:

She blushes, curt'sies, frowns, in short, she
Dreads lest the subject should transport me;
And flying off in search of reason,
Brings prudence back in proper season.
All I shall therefore say (whate'er
I think, is neither here nor there)
Is, that such lips, of looks endearing,
Were form'd for better things than sneering:
Counsel like mine is like a brother's:
My heart is given to some others;
That is to say, unskill'd to cozen,
It shares itself among a dozen.
Marion, adieu! oh, pr'ythee slight not
This warning though it may delight not;
And, lest my precepts be displeasing
To those who think remonstrance teasing,
At once I'll tell thee our opinion
Concerning woman's soft dominion:
Howe'er we gaze with admiration
On eyes of blue or lips carnation,
Howe'er the flowing locks attract us,
Howe'er those beauties may distract us,
Still fickle, we are prone to rove,
These cannot fix our souls to love:
It is not too severe a stricture
To say they form a pretty picture;
But wouldst thou see the secret chain
Which binds us in your humble train,
To hail you queens of all creation,
Know, in a word, 'tis ANIMATION.

MORA.

From high Southannon's distant tower
   Arrived a young and noble dame;
With Kenneth's lands to form her dower,
   Glenalvon's blue-eyed daughter came;

And Oscar claim'd the beauteous bride,
   And Angus on his Oscar smiled:
It soothed the father's feudal pride
   Thus to obtain Glenalvon's child.

Hark to the pibroch's pleasing note!
   Hark to the swelling nuptial song!
In joyous strains the voices float,
   And still the choral peal prolong.

But where is Oscar? sure 'tis late:
   Is this a bridegroom's ardent flame?
While thronging guests and ladies wait,
   Nor Oscar nor his brother came.

At length young Allan join'd the bride:
"Why comes not Oscar," Angus said:
"Is he not here?" the youth replied;
"With me he roved not o'er the glade:

"Perchance, forgetful of the day,
'Tis his to chase the bounding roe;
Or ocean's waves prolong his stay;
Yet Oscar's bark is seldom slow."

"Oh, no!" the anguish'd sire rejoin'd,
"Nor chase nor wave my boy delay;
Would he to Mora seem unkind?
Would aught to her impede his way?"

Three days, three sleepless nights, the Chief
For Oscar search'd each mountain cave;
Then hope is lost; in boundless grief,
His locks in gray-torn ringlets wave.

Days rolled along, the orb of light
Again had run his destined race;
No Oscar bless'd his father's sight,
And sorrow left a fainter trace.

For youthful Allan still remain'd,
And now his father's only joy;
And Mora's heart was quickly gain'd,
For beauty crown'd the fair-hair'd boy.

She thought that Oscar low was laid,
    And Allan's face was wondrous fair;
If Oscar lived, some other maid
    Had claimed his faithless bosom's care.

And Angus said, if one year more
    In fruitless hope was pass'd away,
His fondest scruples should be o'er,
    And he would name their nuptial day.

Again the clan in festive crowd,
    Throng through the gate of Alva's hall:
The sounds of mirth re-echo loud,
    And all their former joy recall.

'Tis noon of night, the pledge goes round,
    The bridegroom's health is deeply quaff'd;
With shouts the vaulted roofs resound,
    And all combine to hail the draught.

Sudden a stranger-chief arose,
    And all the clamorous crowd are hush'd;
And Angus' cheek with wonder glows,
    And Mora's tender bosom blush'd.

"Old man!" he cried, "this pledge is done;
    Thou saw'st 'twas duly drank by me:
It hail'd the nuptials of thy son:
    Now will I claim a pledge from thee.

"While all around is mirth and joy,
 To bless thy Allan's happy lot,
Say, hadst thou ne'er another boy?
 Say, why should Oscar be forgot?"

"Alas!" the hapless sire replied,
 The big tear starting as he spoke,
"When Oscar left my hall, or died,
 This aged heart was almost broke."

"'Tis well," replied the stranger stern,
 And fiercely flash'd his rolling eye:
"Thy Oscar's fate I fain would learn;
 Perhaps the hero did not die.

"Fill high the bowl the table round,
 We will not claim the pledge by stealth;
With wine let every cup be crowned;
 Pledge me departed Oscar's health."

"With all my soul," old Angus said,
 And fill'd his goblet to the brim;
"Here's to my boy! alive or dead,
 I ne'er shall find a son like him."

"Bravely, old man, this health has sped;
 But why does Allan trembling stand?
Come, drink remembrance of the dead,
 And raise thy cup with firmer hand."

The crimson glow of Allan's face
    Was turn'd at once to ghastly hue;
The drops of death each other chase
    Adown in agonizing dew.

Thrice did he raise the goblet high,
    And thrice his lips refused to taste;
For thrice he caught the stranger's eye
    On his with deadly fury placed.

And is it thus a brother hails
    A brother's fond remembrance here?
If thus affection's strength prevails,
    What might we not expect from fear?"

Roused by the sneer, he raised the bowl,
    "Would Oscar now could share our mirth!"
Internal fear appall'd his soul;
    He said, and dashed the cup to earth.

"'Tis he! I hear my murderer's voice!"
    Loud shrieks a darkly gleaming form;
"A murderer's voice!" the roof replies,
    And deeply swells the bursting storm.

Cold was the feast, the revel ceased,
    Who lies upon the stony floor?
Oblivion press'd old Angus' breast,
    At length his life-pulse throbs once more.

" Away, away ! let the leech essay
   To pour the light on Allan's eyes : "
His sand is done,—his race is run ;
   Oh ! never more shall Allan rise !

And whence the dreadful stranger came,
   Or who, no mortal wight can tell ;
But no one doubts the form of flame,
   For Alva's sons knew Oscar well.

Ambition nerved young Allan's hand,
   Exulting demons wing'd his dart :
While Envy waved her burning brand,
   And poured her venom round his heart.

And Mora's eye could Allan move,
   She bade his wounded pride rebel ;
Alas ! that eyes which beamed with love
   Should urge the soul to deeds of hell.

THE MAID OF ATHENS.

Maid of Athens, ere we part,
Give, oh, give me back my heart:
Or, since that has left my breast,
Keep it now, and take the rest!
Hear my vow before I go,
Ζώη μοῦ, σάς ἀγαπῶ.

By those tresses unconfined,
Woo'd by each Ægean wind;
By those lids whose jetty fringe
Kiss thy soft cheeks' blooming tinge;
By those wild eyes like the roe,
Ζώη μοῦ, σάς ἀγαπῶ.

By that lip I long to taste;
By that zone-encircled waist;
By all the token-flowers that tell
What words can never speak so well;
By love's alternate joy and wo,
Ζώη μοῦ, σάς ἀγαπῶ.

THE MAID OF ATHENS.

Maid of Athens! I am gone:
Think of me, sweet! when alone.
Though I fly to Istambol,
Athens holds my heart and soul:
Can I cease to love thee? No!
Ζώη μοῦ, σᾶς ἀγαπῶ.

THE MAID OF SARAGOZA.

Is it for this the Spanish maid, aroused,
Hangs on the willow her unstrung guitar,
And, all unsex'd, the anlace hath espoused,
Sung the loud song, and dared the deed of war?
And she, whom once the semblance of a scar
Appall'd, an owlet's larum chill'd with dread,
Now views the column-scattering bay'net jar,
The falchion flash, and o'er the yet warm dead
Stalks with Minerva's step where Mars might quake to tread.

Ye who shall marvel when you hear her tale,
Oh! had you known her in her softer hour,
Mark'd her black eye that mocks her coal-black veil,
Heard her light, lively tones in Lady's bower,
Seen her long locks that foil the painter's power,
Her fairy form, with more than female grace,
Scarce would you deem that Saragoza's tower
Beheld her smile, in Danger's Gorgon face,
Thin the closed ranks, and lead in Glory's fearful chase.

Her lover sinks—she sheds no ill-timed tear;
Her chief is slain—she fills his fatal post;
Her fellows flee—she checks their base career;
The foe retires—she heads the sallying host:
Who can appease like her a lover's ghost?
Who can avenge so well a leader's fall?
What maid retrieve when man's flush'd hope is lost?
Who hang so fiercely on the flying Gaul,
Foil'd by a woman's hand, before a batter'd wall?

Yet are Spain's maids no race of Amazons,
But form'd for all the witching arts of love:
Though thus in arms they emulate her sons,
And in the horrid phalanx dare to move,
'Tis but the tender fierceness of the dove,
Pecking the hand that hovers o'er her mate:
In softness as in firmness far above
Remoter females, famed for sickening prate;
Her mind is nobler sure, her charms perchance as great.

The seal Love's dimpling finger hath impress'd
Denotes how soft that chin which bears his touch:
Her lips, whose kisses pout to leave their nest,
Bid man be valiant ere he merit such:
Her glance how wildly beautiful! how much
Hath Phœbus woo'd in vain to spoil her cheek,
Which glows yet smoother from his amorous clutch!
Who round the North for paler dames would seek?
How poor their forms appear! how languid, wan, and weak!

INEZ.

I.

Oh never talk again to me
    Of northern climes and British ladies;
It has not been your lot to see,
    Like me, the lovely girl of Cadiz.
Although her eye be not of blue,
    Nor fair her locks like English lasses,
How far its own expressive hue
    The languid azure eye surpasses!

Prometheus-like, from heaven she stole
    The fire, that through those silken lashes
In darkest glances seems to roll,
    From eyes that cannot hide their flashes:
And as along her bosom steal
    In lengthen'd flow her raven tresses,
You'd swear each clustering lock could feel,
    And curl'd to give her neck caresses.

Our English maids are long to woo
    And frigid even in possession;
And if their charms be fair to view,
    Their lips are slow at Love's confession:
But, born beneath a brighter sun,
    For love ordain'd the Spanish maid is,
And who,—when fondly, fairly won,—
    Enchants you like the Girl of Cadiz?

The Spanish maid is no coquette,
    Nor joys to see a lover tremble,
And if she love, or if she hate,
    Alike she knows not to dissemble.
Her heart can ne'er be bought or sold—
    Howe'er it beats, it beats sincerely;
And, though it will not bend to gold,
    'Twill love you long, and love you dearly.

The Spanish girl that meets your love
    Ne'er taunts you with a mock denial,
For every thought is bent to prove
    Her passion in the hour of trial.
When thronging foemen menace Spain,
    She dares the deed and shares the danger;
And should her lover press the plain,
    She hurls the spear, her love's avenger.

And when, beneath the evening star,
    She mingles in the gay Bolero,
Or sings to her attuned guitar
    Of Christian knight, or Moorish hero,

Or counts her beads with fairy hand
　　Beneath the twinkling rays of Hesper,
Or joins devotion's choral band,
　　To chant the sweet and hallow'd vesper;—

In each her charms the heart must move
　　Of all who venture to behold her;
Then let not maids less fair reprove
　　Because her bosom is not colder:
Through many a clime 'tis mine to roam
　　Where many a soft and melting maid is,
But none abroad, and few at home,
　　May match the dark-eyed Girl of Cadiz.

II.

Nay, smile not at my sullen brow;
　　Alas! I cannot smile again:
Yet Heaven avert that ever thou
　　Shouldst weep, and haply weep in vain.

And dost thou ask, what secret wo
　　I bear, corroding joy and youth?
And wilt thou vainly seek to know
　　A pang, e'en thou must fail to soothe?

It is not love, it is not hate,
　　Nor low Ambition's honors lost,
That bids me loathe my present state,
　　And fly from all I prized the most:

It is that weariness which springs
　From all I meet, or hear, or see:
To me no pleasure Beauty brings;
　Thine eyes have scarce a charm for me.

It is that settled, ceaseless gloom
　The fabled Hebrew wanderer bore;
That will not look beyond the tomb,
　But cannot hope for rest before.

What Exile from himself can flee?
　To zones, though more and more remote,
Still, still pursues, where'er I be,
　The blight of life—the demon Thought.

Yet others rapt in pleasure seem,
　And taste of all that I forsake;
Oh! may they still of transport dream,
　And ne'er, at least like me, awake!

Through many a clime 'tis mine to go,
　With many a retrospection cursed;
And all my solace is to know,
　Whate'er betides I've known the worst.

What is that worst? Nay, do not ask—
　In pity from the search forbear:
Smile on—nor venture to unmask
　Man's heart, and view the Hell that's there.

FLORENCE.

I.

Sweet Florence! could another ever share
This wayward, loveless heart, it would be thine:
But check'd by every tie, I may not dare
To cast a worthless offering at thy shrine,
Nor ask so dear a breast to feel one pang for mine.

Thus Harold deem'd, as on that lady's eye
He look'd, and met its beam without a thought,
Save Admiration glancing harmless by:
Love kept aloof, albeit not far remote,
Who knew his votary often lost and caught,
But knew him as his worshipper no more,
And ne'er again the boy his bosom sought:
Since how he vainly urged him to adore,
Well deem'd the little God his ancient sway was o'er.

Fair Florence found, in sooth with some amaze,
One who, 'twas said, still sigh'd to all he saw,
Withstand, unmoved, the lustre of her gaze,

Which others hail'd with real or mimic awe,
Their hope, their doom, their punishment, their law;
All that gay Beauty from her bondsmen claims:
And much she marvell'd that a youth so raw
Nor felt, nor feign'd at least, the oft-told flames,
Which, though sometimes they frown, yet rarely anger dames.

Little knew she that seeming marble heart,
Now mask'd in silence or withheld by pride,
Was not unskilful in the spoiler's art,
And spread its snares licentious far and wide;
Nor from the base pursuit had turn'd aside,
As long as aught was worthy to pursue:
But Harold on such arts no more relied;
And had he doted on those eyes so blue,
Yet never would he join the lover's whining crew.

II.

Oh Lady! when I left the shore,
    The distant shore which gave me birth,
I hardly thought to grieve once more,
    To quit another spot on earth:

Yet here, amidst this barren isle,
    Where panting Nature droops the head,
Where only thou art seen to smile,
    I view my parting hour with dread.

Though far from Albin's craggy shore,
   Divided by the dark blue main;
A few, brief, rolling seasons o'er,
   Perchance I view her cliffs again:

But wheresoe'er I now may roam,
   Through scorching clime, and varied sea,
Though Time restore me to my home,
   I ne'er shall bend mine eyes on thee:

On thee, in whom at once conspire
   All charms which heedless hearts can move,
Whom but to see is to admire,
   And, oh! forgive the word—to love.

Forgive the word, in one who ne'er
   With such a word can more offend;
And since thy heart I cannot share,
   Believe me, what I am, thy friend.

And who so cold as look on thee,
   Thou lovely wanderer, and be less?
Nor be, what man should ever be,
   The friend of Beauty in distress?

Ah! who would think that form had pass'd
   Through Danger's most destructive path,
Had braved the death-wing'd tempest's blast,
   And 'scaped a tyrant's fiercer wrath?

Lady! when I shall view the walls
  Where free Byzantium once arose,
And Stamboul's Oriental halls
  The Turkish tyrants now enclose;

Though mightiest in the lists of fame,
  That glorious city still shall be;
On me 'twill hold a dearer claim,
  As spot of thy nativity:

And though I bid thee now farewell,
  When I behold that wondrous scene,
Since where thou art I may not dwell,
  'Twill soothe to be, where thou hast been.

III.

[WRITTEN IN PASSING THE AMBRACIAN GULF.]

Through cloudless skies, in silvery sheen,
  Full beams the moon on Actium's coast:
And on these waves, for Egypt's queen,
  The ancient world was won and lost.

And now upon the scene I look,
  The azure grave of many a Roman;
Where stern Ambition once forsook
  His wavering crown to follow woman.

Florence! whom I will love as well
  As ever yet was said or sung,
(Since Orpheus sang his spouse from hell,)
  Whilst thou art fair and I am young;

Sweet Florence! those were pleasant times,
  When worlds were staked for ladies' eyes:
Had bards as many realms as rhymes,
  Thy charms might raise new Antonies.

Though Fate forbids such things to be
  Yet, by thine eyes and ringlets curl'd!
I cannot lose a world for thee,
  But would not lose thee for a world.

IV.

While wand'ring through each broken path,
  O'er brake and craggy brow;
While elements exhaust their wrath,
  Sweet Florence, where art thou?

Not on the sea, not on the sea,
  Thy bark hath long been gone:
Oh, may the storm that pours on me,
  Bow down my head alone!

Full swiftly blew the swift Siroc,
  When last I press'd thy lip;
And long ere now, with foaming shock,
  Impell'd thy gallant ship.

Now thou art safe; nay, long ere now
    Hast trod the shore of Spain;
'Twere hard if aught so fair as thou
    Should linger on the main.

And since I now remember thee
    In darkness and in dread,
As in those hours of revelry
    Which mirth and music sped;

Do thou, amid the fair white walls,
    If Cadiz yet be free,
At times from out her latticed halls
    Look o'er the dark blue sea;

Then think upon Calypso's isles,
    Endear'd by days gone by;
To others give a thousand smiles,
    To me a single sigh.

And when the admiring circle mark
    The paleness of thy face,
A half-form'd tear, a transient spark
    Of melancholy grace,

Again thou'lt smile, and blushing shun
    Some coxcomb's raillery;
Nor own for once thou thought'st on one,
    Who ever thinks on thee.

Though smile and sigh alike are vain,
    When sever'd hearts repine,
My spirit flies o'er mount and main,
    And mourns in search of thine.

LIGHT OF THE HAREM.

1.

Here woman's voice is never heard: apart,
And scarce permitted, guarded, veil'd, to move,
She yields to one her person and her heart,
Tamed to her cage, nor feels a wish to rove:
And joyful in a mother's gentlest cares,
For, not unhappy in her master's love,
Blest cares! all other feelings far above!
Herself more sweetly rears the babe she bears,
Who never quits the breast, no meaner passion shares.

II.

They lock them up, and veil, and guard them daily;
  They scarcely can behold their male relations;
So that their moments do not pass so gayly
  As is supposed the case with northern nations;

Confinement, too, must make them look quite palely;
   And as the Turks abhor long conversations,
Their days are either passed in doing nothing,
   Or bathing, nursing, making love, and clothing.

They cannot read, and so don't lisp in criticism;
   Nor write, and so they don't affect the muse;
Were never caught in epigram or witticism,
   Have no romances, sermons, plays, reviews.
In harems learning soon would make a pretty schism!
   But luckily these beauties are no " Blues,"
No bustling Botherbys have they to show 'em
" That charming passage in the last new poem."

The poor dear Musselwomen whom I mention
   Have none of these instructive pleasant people;
And *one* would seem to them a new invention,
   Unknown as bells within a Turkish steeple.
I think 'twould almost be worth while to pension
   (Though best-sown projects very often reap ill)
A missionary author, just to preach
Our Christian usage of the parts of speech.

No chemistry for them unfolds her gases;
   No metaphysics are let loose in lectures;
No circulating library amasses
   Religious novels, moral tales, and strictures
Upon the living manners, as they pass us;
   No exhibition glares with annual pictures;
They stare not on the stars from out their attics,
Nor deal (thank God for that!) in mathematics.

JULIA.

Here the self-torturing sophist, wild Rousseau,
The apostle of affliction, he who threw
Enchantment over passion, and from wo
Wrung overwhelming eloquence, first drew
The breath which made him wretched; yet he knew
How to make madness beautiful, and cast
O'er erring deeds and thoughts a heavenly hue
Of words, like sunbeams, dazzling as they pass'd
The eyes, which o'er them shed tears feelingly and fast.

His love was passion's essence—as a tree
On fire by lightning; with ethereal flame
Kindled he was, and blasted; for to be
Thus, and enamor'd, were in him the same.
But his was not the love of living dame,
Nor of the dead who rise upon our dreams,
But of ideal beauty, which became
In him existence, and o'erflowing teems
Along his burning page, distemper'd though it seems.

This breathed itself to life in Julie, *this*
Invested her with all that's wild and sweet;
This hallow'd, too, the memorable kiss
Which every morn his fever'd lip would greet,
From hers, who but with friendship his would meet;
But to that gentle touch, through brain and breast
Flash'd the thrill'd spirit's love-devouring heat;
In that absorbing sigh perchance more bless'd
Than vulgar minds may be with all they seek possess'd.

THE YOUNG HAIDÉE.

"Μπένω μες 'το' πέριβολι
' Ωραιότατη Χαηδή," &c.

I ENTER thy garden of roses,
   Beloved and fair Haidée,
Each morning where Flora reposes,
   For surely I see her in thee.
Oh, Lovely! thus low I implore thee,
   Receive this fond truth from my tongue,
Which utters its song to adore thee,
   Yet trembles for what it has sung;
As the branch at the bidding of Nature,
   Adds fragrance and fruit to the tree,
Through her eyes, through her every feature
   Shines the soul of the young Haidée.

But the loveliest garden grows hateful
   When Love has abandon'd the bowers;
Bring me hemlock—since mine is ungrateful,
   That herb is more fragrant than flowers.
The poison, when pour'd from the chalice,
   Will deeply embitter the bowl;

But when drunk to escape from thy malice,
    The draught shall be sweet to my soul.
Too cruel! in vain I implore thee
    My heart from these horrors to save:
Will naught to my bosom restore thee?
    Then open the gates of the grave.

As the chief who to combat advances
    Secure of his conquest before,
Thus thou, with those eyes for thy lances,
    Hast pierced through my heart to its core.
Ah, tell me, my soul! must I perish
    By pangs which a smile would dispel?
Would the hope, which thou once bid'st me cherish,
    For torture repay me too well?
Now sad is the garden of roses,
    Beloved but false Haidée!
There Flora all wither'd reposes,
    And mourns o'er thine absence with me.

GENEVRA.

I.

Thine eyes' blue tenderness, thy long fair hair,
   And the wan lustre of thy features—caught
   From contemplation—where serenely wrought,
Seems Sorrow's softness charm'd from its despair—
Have thrown such speaking sadness in thine air,
   That—but I know thy blessed bosom fraught
   With mines of unalloyed and stainless thought—
I should have deem'd thee doom'd to earthly care.
With such an aspect, by his colors blent,
   When from his beauty-breathing pencil born,
(Except that *thou* hast nothing to repent,)
   The Magdalen of Guido saw the morn—
Such seem'st thou—but how much more excellent!
   With naught Remorse can claim—nor Virtue scorn.

II.

Thy cheek is pale with thought, but not from wo,
   And yet so lovely that if Mirth could flush
   Its rose of whiteness with the brightest blush,
My heart would wish away that ruder glow:
And dazzle not thy deep-blue eyes—but, oh!
   While gazing on them sterner eyes will gush,
   And into mine my mother's weakness rush,
Soft as the last drops round heaven's airy bow.
For through thy long dark lashes low depending,
   The soul of melancholy Gentleness
Gleams like a seraph from the sky descending,
   Above all pain, yet pitying all distress;
At once such majesty with sweetness blending,
   I worship more, but cannot love thee less.

LEILA.

Her eye's dark charm 'twere vain to tell!
But gaze on that of the Gazelle,
It will assist thy fancy well;
As large, as languishingly dark;
But Soul beam'd forth in every spark
That darted from beneath the lid,
Bright as the jewel of Giamschid.
Yea, *Soul*, and should our prophet say
That form was naught but breathing clay,
By Alla! I would answer nay;
Though on Al-Sirat's arch I stood,
Which totters o'er the fiery flood,
With Paradise within my view,
And all his Houris beckoning through.
Oh! who young Leila's glance could read
And keep that portion of his creed,
Which saith that woman is but dust,
A soulless toy for tyrant's lust?
On her might Muftis gaze, and own
That through her eye the Immortal shone;

On her fair cheek's unfading hue
The young pomegranate's blossoms strew
Their bloom in blushes ever new :
Her hair in hyacinthine flow,
When left to roll its folds below,
As midst her handmaids in the hall
She stood superior to them all,
Hath swept the marble where her feet
Gleam'd whiter than the mountain sleet
Ere from the cloud that gave it birth
It fell, and caught one stain of earth.
The cygnet nobly walks the water ;
So moved on earth Circassia's daughter,
The loveliest bird of Franguestan !
As rears her crest the ruffled Swan,
 And spurns the wave with wings of pride,
When pass the steps of stranger man
 Along the banks that bound her tide ;
Thus rose fair Leila's whiter neck :—
Thus arm'd with beauty would she check
Intrusion's glance, till Folly's gaze
Shrunk from the charms it meant to praise :
Thus high and graceful was her gait ;
Her heart as tender to her mate ;
Her mate—stern Hassan, who was he?
Alas ! that name was not for thee !
  * * * * *

I hear the sound of coming feet,
But not a voice mine ear to greet ;
More near,—each turban I can scan,
And silver-sheathed ataghan :

The foremost of the band is seen
An Emir by his garb of green:
"Ho! who art thou?" This low salam
Replies, "Of Moslem faith I am."
"The burden ye so gently bear
Seems one that claims your utmost care,
And, doubtless, holds some precious freight,
My humble bark would gladly wait."

"Thou speakest sooth; thy skiff unmoor,
And waft us from the silent shore;
Nay, leave the sail still furl'd, and ply
The nearest oar that's scatter'd by,
And midway to those rocks where sleep
The channel'd waters dark and deep.
Rest from your task—so—bravely done,
Our course has been right swiftly run:
Yet 'tis the longest voyage, I trow,
That one of— * * *

* * * * *

Sullen it plunged, and slowly sank,
The calm wave rippled to the bank;
I watch'd it as it sank, methought
Some motion from the current caught
Bestirr'd it more,—'twas but the beam
That checker'd o'er the living stream:
I gazed, till vanishing from view,
Like lessening pebble it withdrew;
Still less and less, a speck of white
That gemm'd the tide, then mock'd the sight;

And all its hidden secrets sleep,
Known but to Genii of the deep,
Which, trembling in their coral caves,
They dare not whisper to the waves.

  * * * * *

"Yes, Leila sleeps beneath the wave,
But his shall be a redder grave;
Her spirit pointed well the steel
Which taught that felon heart to feel.
He call'd the Prophet, but his power
Was vain against the vengeful Giaour;
He called on Alla—but the word
Arose unheeded or unheard.
Thou Paynim fool! could Leila's prayer
Be pass'd, and thine recorded there?
I watch'd my time, I leagued with these,
The traitor in his turn to seize;
My wrath is wreak'd, the deed is done,
And now I go—but go alone."

  * * *

'Twas then, I tell thee, father! then
I saw her; yes, she lived again;
And shining in her white symar,
As through yon pale gray cloud the star
Which now I gaze on, as on her,
Who look'd and looks far lovelier;
Dimly I view its trembling spark;
To-morrow's night shall be more dark;
And I, before its rays appear,
That lifeless thing the living fear.

I wander, father! for my soul
Is fleeting towards the final goal.
I saw her, friar! and I rose
Forgetful of our former woes;
And rushing from my couch, I dart,
And clasp her to my desperate heart;
I clasp—what is it that I clasp?
No breathing form within my grasp;
No heart that beats reply to mine;
Yet, Leila! yet the form is thine!
And art thou, dearest, changed so much,
As meet my eye, yet mock my touch?
Ah! were thy beauties e'er so cold,
I care not; so my arms enfold
The all they ever wish'd to hold.
Alas! around a shadow press'd,
They shrink upon my lonely breast;
Yet still 'tis there! In silence stands,
And beckons with beseeching hands!
With braided hair, and bright-black eye—
I knew 'twas false—she could not die!
But he is dead! within the dell
I saw him buried where he fell;
He comes not, for he cannot break
From earth; why then art thou awake?
They told me wild waves roll'd above
The face I view, the form I love;
They told me—'twas a hideous tale!
I'd tell it, but my tongue would fail:
If true, and from thine ocean-cave
Thou com'st to claim a calmer grave,

Oh! pass thy dewy fingers o'er
This brow that then will burn no more;
Or place them on my hopeless heart:
But, shape or shade! whate'er thou art,
In mercy ne'er again depart!
Or farther with thee bear my soul
Than winds can waft or waters roll?

ZULEIKA.

FAIR, as the first that fell of womankind,
    When on that dread yet lovely serpent smiling,
Whose image then was stamp'd upon her mind—
    But once beguiled—and ever more beguiling;
Dazzling, as that, oh! too transcendent vision
    To Sorrow's phantom-peopled slumber given,
When heart meets heart again in dreams Elysian,
    And paints the lost on Earth revived in Heaven;
Soft, as the memory of buried love;
Pure, as the prayer which Childhood wafts above;
Was she—the daughter of that rude old Chief,
Who met the maid with tears—but not of grief.

Who hath not proved how feebly words essay
To fix one spark of Beauty's heavenly ray?
Who doth not feel, until his failing sight
Faints into dimness with its own delight,
His changing cheek, his sinking heart confess
The might—the majesty of Loveliness?
Such was Zuleika—such around her shone
The nameless charms unmark'd by her alone;

The light of love, the purity of grace,
The mind, the Music breathing from her face,
The heart whose softness harmonized the whole—
And, oh! that eye was in itself a Soul!

 Her graceful arms in meekness bending
  Across her gently-budding breast;
 At one kind word those arms extending
  To clasp the neck of him who blest
  His child caressing and caress'd,
 Zuleika came—and Giaffir felt
 His purpose half within him melt:
 Not that against her fancied weal
 His heart though stern could ever feel;
 Affection chain'd her to that heart;
 Ambition tore the links apart.

 "Zuleika! child of gentleness!
  How dear this very day must tell,
 When I forget my own distress,
  In losing what I love so well,
  To bid thee with another dwell:
  Another! and a braver man
  Was never seen in battle's van.
We Moslem reck not much of blood;
 But yet the line of Carasman
Unchanged, unchangeable hath stood
 First of the bold Timariot bands
That won and well can keep their lands.
Enough that he who comes to woo
Is kinsman of the Bey Oglou:

His years need scarce a thought employ,
I would not have thee wed a boy.
And thou shalt have a noble dower:
And his and my united power
Will laugh to scorn the death-firman,
Which others tremble but to scan,
And teach the messenger what fate
The bearer of such boon may wait.
And now thou know'st thy father's will;
　All that thy sex hath need to know:
'Twas mine to teach obedience still—
　The way to love, thy lord may show."

In silence bow'd the virgin's head;
　And if her eye was fill'd with tears
That stifled feeling dare not shed,
And changed her cheek from pale to red,
　And red to pale, as through her ears
Those winged words like arrows sped,
　What could such be but maiden fears?
So bright the tear in Beauty's eye,
Love half regrets to kiss it dry;
So sweet the blush of Bashfulness,
Even Pity scarce can wish it less!

　　*　　*　　*　　*　　*　　*

His head was leant upon his hand,
　His eye look'd o'er the dark blue water
That swiftly glides and gently swells
Between the winding Dardanelles;

But yet he saw nor sea nor strand,
Nor even his Pacha's turban'd band
   Mix in the game of mimic slaughter,
Careering cleave the folded felt
With sabre stroke right sharply dealt;
Nor mark'd the javelin-darting crowd,
Nor heard their Ollahs wild and loud—
   He thought but of old Giaffir's daughter!

No word from Selim's bosom broke;
One sigh Zuleika's thought bespoke:
Still gazed he through the lattice grate,
Pale, mute, and mournfully sedate.
To him Zuleika's eye was turn'd,
But little from his aspect learn'd;
Equal her grief, yet not the same;
Her heart confess'd a gentler flame:
But yet that heart, alarm'd or weak,
She knew not why, forbade to speak.
Yet speak she must—but when essay?
" How strange he thus should turn away!
Not thus we e'er before have met;
Not thus shall be our parting yet."
Thrice paced she slowly through the room,
   And watch'd his eye—it still was fix'd:
   She snatch'd the urn wherein was mix'd
The Persian Atar-gul's perfume,
And sprinkled all its odors o'er
The pictured roof and marble floor:
The drops that through his glittering vest
The playful girl's appeal address'd

Unheeded o'er his bosom flew,
As if that breast were marble too.
" What, sullen yet? it must not be—
Oh! gentle Selim, this from thee!"
She saw in curious order set
    The fairest flowers of eastern land—
" He loved them once; may touch them yet,
    If offer'd by Zuleika's hand."
The childish thought was hardly breathed
Before the rose was plucked and wreathed;
The next fond moment saw her seat
Her fairy form at Selim's feet:
" This rose to calm my brother's cares
A message from the Bulbul bears;
It says to-night he will prolong
For Selim's ear his sweetest song;
And though his note is somewhat sad,
He'll try for once a strain more glad,
With some faint hope his falter'd lay
May sing these gloomy thoughts away.

" What! not receive my foolish flower?
    Nay then I am indeed unblest:
On me can thus thy forehead lower?
    And know'st thou not who loves thee best?
Oh, Selim dear! oh, more than dearest!
Say, is it me thou hat'st or fearest?
Come, lay thy head upon my breast,
And I will kiss thee into rest,
Since words of mine, and songs must fail,
Ev'n from my fabled nightingale.

I knew our sire at times was stern,
But this from thee had yet to learn:
Too well I know he loves thee not;
But is Zuleika's love forgot?
Ah! deem I right? the Pacha's plan—
This kinsman Bey of Carasman
Perhaps may prove some foe of thine:
If so, I swear by Mecca's shrine,
If shrines that ne'er approach allow
To woman's step admit her vow,
Without thy free consent, command,
The Sultan should not have my hand!
Think'st thou that I could bear to part
With thee, and learn to halve my heart?
Ah! were I sever'd from thy side,
Where were thy friend—and who my guide?
Years have not seen, Time shall not see
The hour that tears my soul from thee:
Even Azrael, from his deadly quiver
 When flies that shaft, and fly it must,
That parts all else, shall doom forever
 Our hearts to undivided dust!"

MEDORA.

The Sun hath sunk—and, darker than the night,
Sinks with its beam upon the beacon height,
Medora's heart—the third day's come and gone—
With it he comes not—sends not—faithless one!
The wind was fair though light; and storms were none.
Last eve Anselmo's bark return'd, and yet,
His only tidings that they had not met!
Though wild, as now, far different were the tale
Had Conrad waited for that single sail.

The night-breeze freshens—she that day had pass'd
In watching all that Hope proclaim'd a mast;
Sadly she sate—on high—Impatience bore
At last her footsteps to the midnight shore,
And there she wander'd, heedless of the spray
That dash'd her garments oft, and warn'd away:
She saw not—felt not this—nor dared depart,
Nor deem'd it cold—her chill was at her heart;
Till grew such certainty from that suspense—
His very sight had shock'd from life or sense!

It came at last—a sad and shatter'd boat,
Whose inmates first beheld whom first they sought;
Some bleeding—all most wretched—these the few—
Scarce knew they how escaped—*this* all they knew
In silence, darkling, each appear'd to wait
His fellow's mournful guess at Conrad's fate:
Something they would have said; but seem'd to fear
To trust their accents to Medora's ear.
She saw at once, yet sunk not—trembled not—
Beneath that grief, that loneliness of lot;
Within that meek fair form, were feelings high,
That deem'd not till they found their energy.
While yet was Hope—they soften'd—flutter'd—wept:
All lost—that softness died not—but it slept;
And o'er its slumber rose that Strength which said,
"With nothing left to love—there's naught to dread."
'Tis more than nature's; like the burning might
Delirium gathers from the fever's height.

"Silent you stand—nor would I hear you tell
What—speak not—breathe not—for I know it well:
Yet would I ask—almost my lip denies
The—quick your answer—tell me where he lies!"

"Lady! we know not—scarce with life we fled;
But here is one denies that he is dead:
He saw him bound; and bleeding—but alive."

She heard no further—'twas in vain to strive—
So throbb'd each vein—each thought—till then withstood;
Her own dark soul—these words at once subdued;

She totters—falls—and senseless had the wave
Perchance but snatch'd her from another grave;
But that with hands though rude, yet weeping eyes,
They yield such aid as Pity's haste supplies:
Dash o'er her death-like cheek the ocean dew,
Raise—fan—sustain—till life returns anew;
Awake her handmaids, with the matrons leave
That fainting form o'er which they gaze and grieve:
Then seek Anselmo's cavern, to report
The tale too tedious—when the triumph short.

In that wild council words wax'd warm and strange,
With thoughts of ransom, rescue, and revenge;
All, save repose of flight: still lingering there
Breathed Conrad's spirit, and forbade despair;
Whate'er his fate—the breasts he form'd and led,
Will save him living, or appease him dead.
Wo to his foes! there yet survive a few,
Whose deeds are daring, as their hearts are true.

*   *   *   *   *

The lights are high on beacon and from bower,
And 'midst them Conrad seeks Medora's tower:
He looks in vain—'tis strange—and all remark,
Amid so many, hers alone is dark.
'Tis strange—of yore its welcome never fail'd,
Nor now, perchance, extinguish'd, only veil'd.
With the first boat descends he for the shore,
And looks impatient on the lingering oar.
Oh! for a wing beyond the falcon's flight,
To bear him like an arrow to that height!

With the first pause the resting rowers gave,
He waits not—looks not—leaps into the wave,
Strives through the surge, bestrides the beach, and high
Ascends the path familiar to his eye.

He reach'd this turret door—he paused—no sound
Broke from within; and all was night around.
He knock'd, and loudly—footstep nor reply
Announced that any heard or deem'd him nigh;
He knock'd—but faintly—for his trembling hand
Refused to aid his heavy heart's demand.
The portal opens—'tis a well-known face—
But not the form he panted to embrace.
Its lips are silent—twice his own essay'd,
And fail'd to frame the question they delay'd;
He snatch'd the lamp—its light will answer all—
It quits his grasp, expiring in the fall.
He would not wait for that reviving ray—
As soon could he have linger'd there for day;
But, glimmering through the dusky corridore,
Another checkers o'er the shadow'd floor;
His steps the chamber gain—his eyes behold
All that his heart believed not—yet foretold!

He turn'd not—spoke not—sunk not—fix'd his look,
And set the anxious frame that lately shook:
He gazed—how long we gaze despite of pain,
And know, but dare not own, we gaze in vain!
In life itself she was so still and fair,
That death with gentler aspect wither'd there;

And the cold flowers, her colder hand contain'd,
In that last grasp as tenderly were strain'd
As if she scarcely felt, but feign'd a sleep,
And made it almost mockery yet to weep:
The long dark lashes fringed her lids of snow,
And veil'd—thought shrinks from all that lurk'd below—
Oh! o'er the eye Death most exerts his might,
And hurls the spirit from her throne of light;
Sinks those blue orbs in that long last eclipse,
But spares, as yet, the charm around her lips—
Yet, yet they seem as they forbore to smile,
And wished repose—but only for a while;
But the white shroud, and each extended tress,
Long—fair—but spread in utter lifelessness,
Which, late the sport of every summer wind,
Escaped the baffled wreath that strove to bind;
These—and the pale pure cheek, became the bier—
But she is nothing—wherefore is he here?

He ask'd no question—all were answer'd now
By the first glance on that still, marble brow:
It was enough—she died—what reck'd it how?
The love of youth, the hope of better years,
The source of softest wishes, tenderest fears,
The only living thing he could not hate,
Was reft at once—and he deserved his fate,
But did not feel it less;—the good explore,
For peace, those realms where guilt can never soar:
The proud—the wayward—who have fixed below
Their joy, and find this earth enough for wo,

Lose in that one their all—perchance a mite.
But who in patience parts with all delight?
Full many a stoic eye and aspect stern
Mask hearts where grief hath little left to learn;
And many a withering thought lies hid, not lost,
In smiles that least befit who wear them most.

GULNARE.

The midnight pass'd, and to the massy door
A light step came. It paused—it moved once more;
Slow turns the grating bolt and sullen key:
'Tis as his heart foreboded—that fair she!
Whate'er her sins, to him a guardian saint,
And beauteous still as hermit's hope can paint;
Yet changed since last within that cell she came,
More pale her cheek, more tremulous her frame.
On him she cast her dark and hurried eye,
Which spoke before her accents—"Thou must die!
Yes, thou must die—there is but one resource,
The last—the worst—if torture were not worse."

"Lady! I look to none—my lips proclaim
What last proclaim'd they—Conrad still the same.
Why shouldst thou seek an outlaw's life to spare,
And change the sentence I deserve to bear?
Well have I earn'd—nor here alone—the meed
Of Seyd's revenge, by many a lawless deed."

"Why should I seek? because—Oh! didst thou not
Redeem my life from worse than slavery's lot?
Why should I seek?—hath misery made thee blind
To the fond workings of a woman's mind?
And must I say? albeit my heart rebel
With all that woman feels, but should not tell—
Because—despite thy crimes—that heart is moved:
It fear'd thee—thank'd thee—pitied—madden'd—loved.
Reply not—tell not now thy tale again,
Thou lov'st another—and I love in vain;
Though fond as mine her bosom, form more fair,
I rush through peril which she would not dare.
If that thy heart to hers were truly dear,
Were I thine own—thou wert not lonely here:
An outlaw's spouse—and leave her lord to roam!
What hath such gentle dame to do with home?
But speak not now—o'er thine and o'er my head
Hangs the keen sabre by a single thread;
If thou hast courage still, and wouldst be free,
Receive this poniard—rise—and follow me!"

"Ay—in my chains! my steps will gently tread,
With these adornments, o'er each slumbering head!
Thou hast forgot—is this a garb for flight?
Or is that instrument more fit for fight?"

"Misdoubting Corsair! I have gain'd the guard,
Ripe for revolt, and greedy for reward.
A single word of mine removes that chain:
Without some aid how here could I remain?

Well, since we met, hath sped my busy time,
If in aught evil, for thy sake the crime:
The crime—'tis none to punish those of Seyd.
That hated tyrant, Conrad—he must bleed!
I see thee shudder—but my soul is changed—
Wrong'd, spurn'd, reviled—and it shall be avenged—
Accused of what till now my heart disdain'd—
Too faithful, though to bitter bondage chain'd.
Yes, smile!—but he had little cause to sneer,
I was not treacherous then—nor thou too dear:
But he has said it—and the jealous well,
Those tyrants, teasing, tempting to rebel,
Deserve the fate their fretting lips foretell.
I never loved—he bought me—somewhat high—
Since with me came a heart he could not buy.
I was a slave unmurmuring: he hath said,
But for his rescue I with thee had fled.
'Twas false thou know'st—but let such augurs rue,
Their words are omens Insult renders true.
Nor was thy respite granted to my prayer;
This fleeting grace was only to prepare
New torments for thy life, and my despair.
Mine too he threatens; but his dotage still
Would fain reserve me for his lordly will:
When wearier of these fleeting charms and me,
There yawns the sack—and yonder rolls the sea!
What, am I then a toy for dotard's play,
To wear but till the gilding frets away?
I saw thee—loved thee—owe thee all—would save,
If but to show how grateful is a slave.

But had he not thus menaced fame and life,
(And well he keeps his oaths pronounced in strife,)
I still had saved thee—but the Pacha spared.
Now I am all thine own—for all prepared:
Thou lov'st me not—nor know'st—or but the worst.
Alas! this love—that hatred are the first—
Oh! couldst thou prove my truth, thou wouldst not start,
Nor fear the fire that lights an Eastern heart;
'Tis now the beacon of thy safety—now
It points within the port a Mainote prow:
But in one chamber, where our path must lead,
There sleeps—he must not wake—the oppressor Seyd!"

"Gulnare—Gulnare—I never felt till now
My abject fortune, wither'd fame so low:
Seyd is mine enemy: had swept my band
From earth with ruthless but with open hand,
And therefore came I, in my bark of war,
To smite the smiter with a scimitar;
Such is my weapon—not the secret knife—
Who spares a woman's seeks not slumber's life.
Thine saved I gladly, Lady, not for this—
Let me not deem that mercy shown amiss.
Now fare thee well—more peace be with thy breast!
Night wears apace—my last of earthly rest!"

"Rest! rest! by sunrise must thy sinews shake,
And thy limbs writhe around the ready stake.
I heard the order—saw—I will not see—
If thou wilt perish, I will fall with thee.

My life—my love—my hatred—all below
Are on this cast—Corsair! 'tis but a blow!
Without it flight were idle—how evade
His sure pursuit? my wrongs too unrepaid,
My youth disgraced—the long, long wasted years,
One blow shall cancel with our future fears;
But since the dagger suits thee less than brand,
I'll try the firmness of a female hand.
The guards are gain'd—one moment all were o'er—
Corsair! we meet in safety or no more;
If errs my feeble hand, the morning cloud
Will hover o'er thy scaffold, and my shroud.

She turn'd, and vanish'd ere he could reply;
But his glance follow'd far with eager eye;
And gathering, as he could, the links that bound
His form, to curl their length, and curb their sound,
Since bar and bolt no more his steps preclude,
He, fast as fetter'd limbs allow, pursued.
'Twas dark and winding, and he knew not where
That passage led; nor lamp nor guard were there:
He sees a dusky glimmering—shall he seek
Or shun that ray so indistinct and weak?
Chance guides his steps—a freshness seems to bear
Full on his brow, as if from morning air—
He reach'd an open gallery—on his eye
Gleam'd the last star of night, the clearing sky:
Yet scarcely heeded these—another light
From a lone chamber struck upon his sight.
Towards it he moved; a scarcely closing door
Reveal'd the ray within, but nothing more.

With hasty step a figure outward pass'd,
Then paused—and turn'd—and paused—'tis She at last!
No poniard in that hand—nor sign of ill—
"Thanks to that softening heart—she could not kill!"
Again he look'd, the wildness of her eye
Starts from the day abrupt and fearfully.
She stopp'd—threw back her dark far-floating hair,
That nearly veil'd her face and bosom fair:
As if she late had bent her leaning head
Above some object of her doubt or dread.
They meet—upon her brow—unknown—forgot
Her hurrying hand had left—'twas but a spot—
Its hue was all he saw, and scarce withstood—
Oh! slight but certain pledge of crime—'tis blood!

KALED.

AND Lara called his page, and went his way—
Well could that stripling word or sign obey:
His only follower from those climes afar,
Where the soul glows beneath a brighter star;
For Lara left the shore from whence he sprung
In duty patient, and sedate, though young;
Silent as him he served, his faith appears
Above his station, and beyond his years.
Though not unknown the tongue of Lara's land,
In such from him he rarely heard command;
But fleet his step, and clear his tones would come,
When Lara's lip breathed forth the words of home:
Those accents, as his native mountains dear,
Awake their absent echoes in his ear,
Friends', kindred's, parents', wonted voice recall,
Now lost, abjured, for one—his friend, his all:
For him earth now disclosed no other guide;
What marvel then he rarely left his side?

Light was his form, and darkly delicate
That brow whereon his native sun had sate,
But had not marr'd, though in his beams he grew,
The cheek where oft the unbidden blush shone through;
Yet not such blush as mounts when health would show
All the heart's hue in that delighted glow;
But 'twas a hectic tint of secret care
That for a burning moment fever'd there;
And the wild sparkle of his eye seem'd caught
From high, and lighten'd with electric thought,
Though its black orb those long low lashes' fringe
Had temper'd with a melancholy tinge;
Yet less of sorrow than of pride was there,
Or, if 'twere grief, a grief that none should share:
And pleased not him the sports that please his age,
The tricks of youth, the frolics of the page;
For hours on Lara he would fix his glance,
As all-forgotten in that watchful trance;
And from his chief withdrawn, he wander'd lone,
Brief were his answers, and his qestions none;
His walk the wood, his sport some foreign book;
His resting-place the bank that curbs the brook:
He seem'd, like him he served, to live apart
From all that lures the eye, and fills the heart;
To know no brotherhood, and take from earth
No gift beyond that bitter boon—our birth.

If aught he loved, 'twas Lara; but was shown
His faith in reverence and in deeds alone;
In mute attention; and his care, which guess'd
Each wish, fulfill'd it ere the tongue express'd.

Still there was haughtiness in all he did,
A spirit deep that brook'd not to be chid;
His zeal, though more than that of servile hands,
In act alone obeys, his air commands;
As if 'twas Lara's less than *his* desire
That thus he served, but surely not for hire.
Slight were the tasks enjoin'd him by his lord,
To hold the stirrup, or to bear the sword;
To tune his lute, or, if he will'd it more,
On tomes of other times and tongues to pore;
But ne'er to mingle with the menial train,
To whom he show'd nor deference nor disdain,
But that well-worn reserve which proved he knew
No sympathy with that familiar crew:
His soul, whate'er his station or his stem,
Could bow to Lara, not descend to them.
Of higher birth he seem'd, and better days,
Nor mark of vulgar toil that hand betrays,
So femininely white it might bespeak
Another sex, when match'd with that smooth cheek,
But for his garb, and something in his gaze,
More wild and high than woman's eye betrays;
A latent fierceness that far more became
His fiery climate than his tender frame:
True, in his words it broke not from his breast,
But from his aspect might be more than guess'd.
Kaled his name, though rumor said he bore
Another ere he left his mountain shore;
For sometimes he would hear, however nigh,
That name repeated loud without reply,

As unfamiliar, or, if roused again,
Start to the sound, as but remember'd then;
Unless 'twas Lara's wonted voice that spake;
For then, ear, eyes, and heart would all awake.

JEPHTHA'S DAUGHTER.

Since our Country, our God—oh, my sire!
Demand that thy Daughter expire;
Since thy triumph was bought by thy vow—
Strike the bosom that's bared for thee now!

And the voice of my mourning is o'er,
And the mountains behold me no more!
If the hand that I love lay me low,
There cannot be pain in the blow!

And of this, oh, my Father! be sure—
That the blood of thy child is as pure
As the blessing I beg ere it flow,
And the last thought that soothes me below.

Though the virgins of Salem lament,
Be the judge and the hero unbent!
I have won the great battle for thee,
And my father and country are free!

When this blood of thy giving hath gush'd—
When the voice that thou lovest is hush'd,
Let my memory still be thy pride,
And forget not I smiled as I died!

PARISINA.

It is the hour when from the boughs
   The nightingale's high note is heard;
It is the hour when lovers' vows
   Seem sweet in every whisper'd word;
And gentle winds, and waters near,
Make music to the lonely ear.
Each flower the dews have lightly wet,
And in the sky the stars are met,
And on the wave is deeper blue,
And on the leaf a browner hue,
And in the heaven that clear obscure,
So softly dark, and darkly pure,
Which follows the decline of day,
As twilight melts beneath the moon away.

But it is not to list to the waterfall
That Parisina leaves her hall,
And it is not to gaze on the heavenly light
That the lady walks in the shadow of night,

And if she sits in Este's bower,
'Tis not for the sake of its full-blown flower—
She listens—but not for the nightingale—
Though her ear expects as soft a tale.
There glides a step through the foliage thick,
And her cheek grows pale—and her heart beats quick.
There whispers a voice through the rustling leaves,
And her blush returns, and her bosom heaves:
A moment more—and they shall meet—
'Tis past—her lover 's at her feet.

And what unto them is the world beside,
With all its change of time and tide?
Its living things—its earth and sky—
Are nothing to their mind and eye.
And heedless as the dead are they
   Of aught around, above, beneath;
As if all else had pass'd away,
   They only for each other breathe;
Their very sighs are full of joy
   So deep, that did it decay,
That happy madness would destroy
   The hearts which feel its fiery sway.
Of guilt, of peril, do they deem
In that tumultuous tender dream?
Who that have felt that passion's power,
Or paused, or fear'd in such an hour?
Or thought how brief such moments last?
But yet—they are already pass'd!
Alas! we must awake before
We know such vision comes no more.

   *   *   *   *   *

She stood, I said, all pale and still,
The living cause of Hugo's ill:
Her eyes unmoved, but full and wide,
Not once had turn'd to either side—
Nor once did those sweet eyelids close,
Or shade the glance o'er which they rose,
But round their orbs of deepest blue
The circling white dilated grew—
And there with glassy gaze she stood
As ice were in her curdled blood,
But every now and then a tear
  So large and slowly gather'd slid
  From the long dark fringe of that fair lid,
It was a thing to see, not hear!
And those who saw, it did surprise,
Such drops could fall from human eyes.
To speak she thought—the imperfect note
Was choked within her swelling throat,
Yet seem'd in that low hollow groan
Her whole heart gushing in the tone.
It ceased—again she thought to speak,
Then burst her voice in one long shriek,
And to the earth she fell like stone
Or statue from its base o'erthrown,
More like a thing that ne'er had life,—
A monument of Azo's wife,—
Than her, that living guilty thing,
Whose every passion was a sting,
Which urged to guilt, but could not bear
That guilt's detection and despair.

But yet she lived—and all too soon
Recover'd from that death-like swoon—
But scarce to reason—every sense
Had been o'erstrung by pangs intense,
And each frail fibre of her brain
(As bowstrings, when relax'd by rain,
The erring arrow launch aside)
Sent forth her thoughts all wild and wide—
The past a blank, the future black,
With glimpses of a dreary track,
Like lightning on the desert path,
When midnight storms are mustering wrath.
She fear'd—she felt that something ill
Lay on her soul, so deep and chill—
That there was sin and shame she knew;
That some one was to die—but who?
She had forgotten:—did she breathe?
Could this be still the earth beneath,
The sky above, and men around;
Or were they fiends who now so frown'd
On one, before whose eyes each eye
Till then had smiled in sympathy?
All was confused and undefined
To her all-jarr'd and wandering mind;
A chaos of wild hopes and fears:
And now in laughter, now in tears,
But madly still in each extreme,
She strove with that convulsive dream;
For so it seem'd on her to break:
Oh! vainly must she strive to wake!

ASTARTE.

MANFRED.
Yet there was one——

WITCH.
Spare not thyself—proceed.

MANFRED.
She was like me in lineaments—her eyes,
Her hair, her features, all, to the very tone
Even of her voice, they said were like to mine;
But soften'd all, and temper'd into beauty:
She had the same lone thoughts and wanderings,
The quest of hidden knowledge, and a mind
To comprehend the universe: nor these
Alone, but with them gentler powers than mine,
Pity, and smiles, and tears—which I had not;
And tenderness—but that I had for her;
Humility—and that I never had.
Her faults were mine—her virtues were her own—
I loved her, and destroy'd her!

Witch.

With thy hand?

Manfred.

Not with my hand, but heart—which broke her heart—
It gazed on mine, and wither'd. I have shed
Blood, but not hers—and yet her blood was shed.

* * * * * * * *

[*The Phantom of* Astarte *rises and stands in the midst.*]

Can this be death? there's bloom upon her cheek;
But now I see it is no living hue,
But a strange hectic—like the unnatural red
Which Autumn plants upon the perish'd leaf.
It is the same—Oh, God! that I should dread
To look upon the same—Astarte!—No,
I cannot speak to her—but bid her speak—
Forgive me or condemn me.

Nemesis.

By the power which hath broken
 The grave which inthrall'd thee,
Speak to him who hath spoken,
 Or those who have call'd thee!

Manfred.

She is silent,
And in that silence I am more than answered.

Nemesis.

My power extends no further. Prince of air!
It rests with thee alone—command her voice.

ARIEL.
Spirit—obey this sceptre!

NEMESIS.
Silent still!
She is not of our order, but belongs
To the other powers. Mortal! thy quest is vain,
And we are baffled also.

MANFRED.
Hear me, hear me—
Astarte! my beloved! speak to me:
I have so much endured—so much endure—
Look on me! the grave hath not changed thee more
Than I am changed for thee. Thou lovedst me
Too much, as I loved thee: we were not made
To torture thus each other, though it were
The deadliest sin to love as we have loved.
I know not what I ask, nor what I seek:
I feel but what thou art—and what I am; ·
And I would hear yet once before I perish
The voice which was my music—Speak to me!
For I have call'd on thee in the still night,
Startled the slumbering birds from the hush'd boughs,
And woke the mountain wolves, and made the caves
Acquainted with thy vainly echo'd name,
Which answer'd me—many things answer'd me—
Spirits and men—but thou wert silent all.
Yet speak to me! I have outwatch'd the stars,
And gazed o'er heaven in vain in search of thee.
Speak to me! I have wander'd o'er the earth,
And never found thy likeness—Speak to me!

Look on the fiends around—they feel for me:
I fear them not, and feel for thee alone—
Speak to me! though it be in wrath;—but say—
I reck not what—but let me hear thee once—
This once—once more!

Phantom of Astarte.

Manfred!

Manfred.

Say, say on—
I live but in the sound—it is thy voice!

Phantom.

Manfred! To-morrow ends thine earthly ills.
Farewell!

Manfred.

Yet one word more—am I forgiven?

Phantom.

Farewell!

Manfred.

Say, shall we meet again?

Phantom.

Farewell!

Manfred.

One word for mercy! Say, thou lovest me.

Phantom.

Manfred!

[*The Spirit of* Astarte *disappears.*

LEONORA D'ESTE.

They call'd me mad—and why?
Oh Leonora! wilt not *thou* reply?
I was indeed delirious in my heart
To lift my love so lofty as thou art;
But still my phrensy was not of the mind;
I knew my fault, and feel my punishment
Not less because I suffer it unbent.
That thou wert beautiful, and I not blind,
Hath been the sin which shuts me from mankind;
But let them go, or torture as they will,
My heart can multiply thine image still;
Successful love may sate itself away,
The wretched are the faithful; 'tis their fate
To have all feeling save the one decay,
And every passion into one dilate,
As rapid rivers into ocean pour;
But ours is fathomless, and hath no shore.

* * * * * *

Look on a love which knows not to despair,

But all unquench'd is still my better part,
Dwelling deep in my shut and silent heart,
As dwells the gather'd lightning in its cloud,
Encompass'd with its dark and rolling shroud,
Till struck,—forth flies the all-ethereal dart!
And thus at the collision of thy name
The vivid thought still flashes through my frame,
And for a moment all things as they were
Flit by me;—they are gone—I am the same.
And yet my love without ambition grew;
I knew thy state, my station, and I knew
A Princess was no love-mate for a bard;
I told it not, I breathed it not, it was
Sufficient to itself, its own reward;
And if my eyes reveal'd it, they, alas!
Were punish'd by the silentness of thine,
And yet I did not venture to repine.
Thou wert to me a crystal-girded shrine,
Worshipp'd at holy distance, and around
Hallow'd and meekly kiss'd the saintly ground;
Not for thou wert a princess, but that Love
Had robed thee with a glory, and array'd
Thy lineaments in beauty that dismay'd—
Oh! not dismay'd—but awed, like One above!
And in that sweet severity there was
A something which all softness did surpass—
The very love which lock'd me to my chain
Hath lighten'd half its weight; and for the rest,
Though heavy, lent me vigor to sustain,
And look to thee with undivided breast,
And foil the ingenuity of Pain.

LAURA.

She was not old, nor young, nor at the years
   Which certain people call a "*certain age*,"
Which yet the most uncertain age appears,
   Because I never heard, nor could engage
A person yet by prayers, or bribes, or tears,
   To name, define by speech, or write on page,
The period meant precisely by that word,—
Which surely is exceedingly absurd.

Laura was blooming still, had made the best
   Of time, and time return'd the compliment,
And treated her genteelly, so that, dress'd,
   She look'd extremely well where'er she went;
A pretty woman is a welcome guest,
   And Luara's brow a frown had rarely bent;
Indeed she shone all smiles, and seem'd to flatter
Mankind with her black eyes for looking at her.

Laura, when dress'd, was (as I sang before)
   A pretty woman as was ever seen,
Fresh as the Angel o'er a new inn door,
   Or frontispiece of a new Magazine,

With all the fashions which the last month wore,
   Color'd, and silver paper leaved between
That and the title-page, for fear the press
Should soil with parts of speech the parts of dress.

Now Laura moves along the joyous crowd,
   Smiles in her eyes, and simpers on her lips;
To some she whispers, others speaks aloud;
   To some she courtsies, and to some she dips,
Complains of warmth, and this complaint avow'd,
   Her lover brings the lemonade, she sips;
She then surveys, condemns, but pities still
Her dearest friends for being dress'd so ill.

One has false curls, another too much paint,
   A third—where did she buy that frightful turban?
A fourth's so pale she fears she's going to faint,
   A fifth's look's vulgar, dowdyish, and suburban,
A sixth's white silk has got a yellow taint,
   A seventh's thin muslin surely will be her bane,
And lo! an eighth appears,—" I'll see no more!"
For fear, like Banquo's king, they reach a score.

Meantime, while she was thus at others gazing,
   Others were levelling their looks at her;
She heard the men's half-whisper'd mode of praising,
   And till 'twas done, determined not to stir;
The women only thought it quite amazing
   That, at her time of life, so many were
Admirers still,—but men are so debased,
Those brazen creatures always suit their taste.

THERESA.

Theresa's form—
Methinks it glides before me now,
Between me and yon chestnut's bough,
The memory is so quick and warm;
And yet I find no words to tell
The shape of her I loved so well:
She had the Asiatic eye,
    Such as our Turkish neighborhood,
    Hath mingled with our Polish blood,
Dark as above us is the sky;
But through it stole a tender light,
Like the first moonrise of midnight;
Large, dark, and swimming in the stream,
Which seem'd to melt to its own beam:
All love, half languor, and half fire,
Like saints that at the stake expire,
And lift their raptured looks on high,
As though it were a joy to die.
A brow like a midsummer lake,
    Transparent with the sun therein,

When waves no murmur dare to make,
　　And heaven beholds her face within.
A cheek and lip—but why proceed?
　　I loved her then—I love her still;
And such as I am, love indeed
　　In fierce extremes—in good and ill.
But still we love even in our rage,
And haunted to our very age
With the vain shadow of the past,
As is Mazeppa to the last.

We met—we gazed—I saw, and sigh'd,
She did not speak, and yet replied;
There are ten thousand tones and signs
We hear and see, but none defines—
Involuntary sparks of thought,
Which strike from out the heart o'erwrought,
And form a strange intelligence,
Alike mysterious and intense,
Which link the burning chain that binds,
Without their will, young hearts and minds;
Conveying, as the electric wire,
We know not how, the absorbing fire.—
I saw, and sigh'd—in silence wept,
And still reluctant distance kept,
Until I was made known to her,
And we might then and there confer
Without suspicion—then, even then,
　　I long'd, and was resolved to speak;
But on my lips they died again,
　　The accents tremulous and weak,

Until one hour.—There is a game,
  A frivolous and foolish play,
  Wherewith we while away the day;
It is—I have forgot the name—
And we to this, it seems were set,
By some strange chance which I forget:
I reck'd not if I won or lost,
  It was enough for me to be
  So near to hear, and oh! to see
The being whom I loved the most.—
I watch'd her as a sentinel,
(May ours this dark night watch as well!)
  Until I saw, and thus it was,
That she was pensive, nor perceived
Her occupation, nor was grieved
Nor glad to lose or gain; but still
Play'd on for hours, as if her will
Yet bound her to the place, though not
That hers might be the winning lot.

  Then through my brain the thought did pass
Even as a flash of lightning there,
That there was something in her air
Which would not doom me to despair;
And on the thought my words broke forth,
  All incoherent as they were—
Their eloquence was little worth,
But yet she listen'd—'tis enough—
  Who listens once will listen twice;
  Her heart, be sure, is not of ice,
And one refusal no rebuff.

I loved and was beloved again—
   They tell me, sire, you never knew
   Those gentle frailties; if 'tis true,
I shorten all my joy or pain;
To you 'twould seem absurd as vain;
But all men are not born to reign,
Or o'er their passions, or as you
Thus o'er themselves and nations too.
I am—or rather *was*—a prince,
   A chief of thousands, and could lead
   Them on where each would foremost bleed;
But could not o'er myself evince
The like control—But to resume:
   I loved, and was beloved again;
In sooth, it is a happy doom,
   But yet where happiest ends in pain.—
We met in secret, and the hour
Which led me to that lady's bower
Was fiery Expectation's dower.
My days and nights were nothing—all
Except that hour which doth recall
In the long lapse from youth to age
   No other like itself—I'd give
   The Ukraine back again to live
It o'er once more—and be a page,
The happy page, who was the lord
Of one soft heart, and his own sword,
And had no other gem nor wealth
Save nature's gift of youth and health.

BEATRICE.

ONCE more in man's frail world; which I had left
  So long that 'twas forgotten; and I feel
  The weight of clay again,—too soon bereft
Of the immortal vision which could heal
  My earthly sorrows, and to God's own skies
  Lift me from that deep gulf without repeal,
Where late my ears rung with the damned cries
  Of souls in hopeless bale; and from that place
  Of lesser torment, whence men may arise
Pure from the fire to join the angelic race;
  Midst whom my own bright Beatricë bless'd
  My spirit with her light; and to the base
Of the eternal Triad! first, last, best,
  Mysterious, three, sole, infinite, great God!
  Soul universal! led the mortal guest,
Unblasted by the glory, though he trod
  From star to star to reach the almighty throne.
  Oh Beatricë! whose sweet limbs the sod

So long hath press'd, and the cold marble stone,
　　Thou sole pure seraph of my earliest love,
　　Love so ineffable, and so alone,
That naught on earth could more my bosom move,
　　And meeting thee in heaven was but to meet
　　That without which my soul, like the arkless dove,
Had wander'd still in search of, nor her feet
　　Relieved her wing till found; without thy light
　　My paradise had still been incomplete.
Since my tenth sun gave summer to my sight
　　Thou wert my life, the essence of my thought,
　　Loved ere I knew the name of love, and bright
Still in these dim old eyes, now overwrought
　　With the world's war, and years, and banishment,
　　And tears for thee, by other woes untaught;
For mine is not a nature to be bent
　　By tyrannous faction, and the brawling crowd,
　　And though the long, long conflict hath been spent
In vain, and never more, save when the cloud
　　Which overhangs the Apennine, my mind's eye
　　Pierces to fancy Florence, once so proud
Of me, can I return, though but to die,
　　Unto my native soil, they have not yet
　　Quench'd the old exile's spirit, stern and high.

ANGIOLINA.

[ANGIOLINA AND MARIANNA, *afterwards* FALIERO.]

ANGIOLINA.

'TWAS a gross insult; but I heed it not
For the rash scorner's falsehood in itself,
But for the effect, the deadly deep impression
Which it has made upon Faliero's soul,
The proud, the fiery, the austere—austere
To all save me: I tremble when I think
To what it may conduct.

MARIANNA.
Assuredly
The Doge cannot suspect you?

ANGIOLINA.
Suspect *me!*
Why Steno dared not: when he scrawl'd his lie,
Grovelling by stealth in the moon's glimmering light,
His own still conscience smote him for the act,
And every shadow on the walls frown'd shame
Upon his coward calumny.

MARIANNA.

'Twere fit
He should be punish'd grievously.

ANGIOLINA.

He is so.

MARIANNA.

What! is the sentence pass'd? is he condemn'd?

ANGIOLINA.

I know not that, but he has been detected.

MARIANNA.

And deem you this enough for such foul scorn?

ANGIOLINA.

I would not be a judge in my own cause,
Nor do I know what sense of punishment
May reach the soul of ribalds such as Steno;
But if his insults sink no deeper in
The minds of the inquisitors than they
Have ruffled mine, he will, for all acquittance,
Be left to his own shamelessness or shame.

MARIANNA.

Some sacrifice is due to slander'd virtue.

ANGIOLINA.

Why, what is virtue if it needs a victim?
Or if it must depend upon men's words?
The dying Roman said, " 'twas but a name : "

    It were indeed no more, if human breath
Could make or mar it.

MARIANNA.
Yet full many a dame,
Stainless and faithful, would feel all the wrong
Of such a slander; and less rigid ladies,
Such as abound in Venice, would be loud
And all-inexorable in their cry
For justice.

ANGIOLINA.
This but proves it is the name
And not the quality they prize: the first
Have found it a hard task to hold their honor,
If they require it to be blazon'd forth;
And those who have not kept it, seek its seeming
As they would look out for an ornament
Of which they feel the want, but not because
They think it so; they live in others' thoughts,
And would seem honest, as they must seem fair.

MARIANNA.
You have strange thoughts for a patrician dame.

ANGIOLINA.
And yet they were my father's; with his name,
The sole inheritance he left.

MARIANNA.
You want none;
Wife to a prince, the chief of the Republic.

ANGIOLINA.

I should have sought none though a peasant's bride,
But feel not less the love and gratitude
Due to my father, who bestow'd my hand
Upon his early, tried, and trusted friend,
The Count Val di Marino, now our Doge.

MARIANNA.

And with that hand did he bestow your heart?

ANGIOLINA.

He did so, or it had not been bestow'd.

MARIANNA.

Yet this strange disproportion in your years,
And, let me add, disparity of tempers,
Might make the world doubt whether such a union
Could make you wisely, permanently, happy.

ANGIOLINA.

The world will think with worldlings; but my heart
Has still been in my duties, which are many,
But never difficult.

MARIANNA.

And do you love him?

ANGIOLINA.

I love all noble qualities which merit
Love, and I loved my father, who first taught me
To single out what we should love in others,
And to subdue all tendency to lend
The best and purest feelings of our nature

To baser passions. He bestow'd my hand
Upon Faliero: he had known him noble,
Brave, generous; rich in all the qualities
Of soldier, citizen, and friend; in all
Such have I found him as my father said.
His faults are those that dwell in the high bosoms
Of men who have commanded; too much pride,
And the deep passions fiercely foster'd by
The uses of patricians, and a life
Spent in the storms of state and war; and also
From the quick sense of honor, which becomes
A duty to a certain sign, a vice
When overstrain'd, and this I fear in him.
And then he has been rash from his youth upwards,
Yet temper'd by redeeming nobleness
In such sort, that the wariest of republics
Has lavish'd all its chief employs upon him,
From his first fight to his last embassy,
From which on his return the Dukedom met him.

MARIANNA.

But previous to this marriage, had your heart
Ne'er beat for any of the noble youth,
Such as in years had been more meet to match
Beauty like yours? or since have you ne'er seen
One, who, if your fair hand were still to give,
Might now pretend to Loredano's daughter?

ANGIOLINA.

I answer'd your first question when I said
I married.

MARIANNA.
And the second?

ANGIOLINA.
Needs no answer.

MARIANNA.
I pray your pardon, if I have offended.

ANGIOLINA.
I feel no wrath, but some surprise: I knew not
That wedded bosoms could permit themselves
To ponder upon what they *now* might choose,
Or aught save their past choice.

MARIANNA.
'Tis their past choice
That far too often makes them deem they would
Now choose more wisely, could they cancel it.

ANGIOLINA.
It may be so. I knew not of such thoughts.

MARIANNA.
Here comes the Doge—shall I retire?

ANGIOLINA.
It may
Be better you should quit me; he seems wrapp'd
In thought.—How pensively he takes his way!
[*Exit* MARIANNA.
[*Enter the* DOGE *and* PIETRO.]
DOGE, (*musing*.)
There is a certain Philip Calendaro
Now in the Arsenal, who holds command

Of eighty men, and has great influence
Besides on all the spirits of his comrades:
This man, I hear, is bold and popular,
Sudden and daring, and yet secret; 'twould
Be well that he were won: I needs must hope
That Israel Bertuccio has secured him,
But fain would be——

PIETRO.
My lord, pray pardon me
For breaking in upon your meditation;
The Senator Bertuccio, your kinsman,
Charged me to follow and inquire your pleasure
To fix an hour when he may speak with you.

DOGE.
At sunset.—Stay a moment—let me see—
Say in the second hour of night.　　　[*Exit* PIETRO.

ANGIOLINA.
My lord!

DOGE.
My dearest child, forgive me—why delay
So long approaching me?—I saw you not.

ANGIOLINA.
You were absorb'd in thought, and he who now
Has parted from you might have words of weight
To bear you from the senate.

DOGE.
From the senate?

ANGIOLINA.
I would not interrupt him in his duty
And theirs.

DOGE.
The senate's duty! you mistake;
'Tis we who owe all service to the senate.

ANGIOLINA.
I thought the Duke had held command in Venice.

DOGE.
He shall.—But let that pass.—We will be jocund.
How fares it with you? have you been abroad?
The day is overcast, but the calm wave
Favors the gondolier's light skimming oar;
Or have you held a levee of your friends?
Or has your music made you solitary?
Say—is there aught that you would will within
The little sway now left the Duke? or aught
Of fitting splendor, or of honest pleasure,
Social or lonely, that would glad your heart,
To compensate for many a dull hour, wasted
On an old man oft moved with many cares?
Speak and 'tis done.

ANGIOLINA.
You're ever kind to me—
I have nothing to desire, or to request,
Except to see you oftener and calmer.

DOGE.
Calmer?

ANGIOLINA.

Ay, calmer, my good lord.—Ah, why
Do you still keep apart and walk alone,
And let such strong emotions stamp your brow,
As not betraying their full import, yet
Disclose too much?

DOGE.

Disclose too much!—of what?
What is there to disclose?

ANGIOLINA.
     A heart so ill
At ease.

DOGE.

'Tis nothing, child.—But in the state
You know what daily cares oppress all those
Who govern this precarious commonwealth;
Now suffering from the Genoese without,
And malecontents within—'tis this which makes me
More pensive and less tranquil than my wont.

ANGIOLINA.

Yet this existed long before, and never
Till in these late days did I see you thus.
Forgive me; there is something at your heart
More than the mere discharge of public duties,
Which long use and a talent like to yours
Have render'd light, nay, a necessity,
To keep your mind from stagnating. 'Tis not
In hostile states, nor perils, thus to shake you;

You who have stood all storms and never sunk,
And climb'd up to the pinnacle of power
And never fainted by the way, and stand
Upon it, and can look down steadily
Along the depth beneath, and ne'er feel dizzy.
Were Genoa's galleys riding in the port,
Were civil fury raging in Saint Mark's,
You are not to be wrought on, but would fall,
As you have risen, with an unalter'd brow—
Your feelings now are of a different kind;
Something has stung your pride, not patriotism.

     Doge.
Pride! Angiolina? Alas! none is left me.

     Angiolina.
Yes—the same sin that overthrew the angels,
And of all sins most easily besets
Mortals the nearest to the angelic nature:
The vile are only vain; the great are proud.

     Doge.
I *had* the pride of honor, of *your* honor,
Deep at my heart——But let us change the theme.

     Angiolina.
Ah no!—As I have ever shared your kindness
In all things else, let me not be shut out
From your distress: were it of public import,
You know I never sought, would never seek
To win a word from you; but feeling now
Your grief is private, it belongs to me

To lighten or divide it. Since the day
When foolish Steno's ribaldry detected
Unfix'd your quiet, you are greatly changed,
And I would soothe you back to what you were.

DOGE.
To what I was!—Have you heard Steno's sentence?

ANGIOLINA.
No.

DOGE.
A month's arrest.

ANGIOLINA.
Is it not enough?

DOGE.
Enough!—yes, for a drunken galley-slave,
Who, stung by stripes, may murmur at his master;
But not for a deliberate, false, cool villain,
Who stains a lady's and a prince's honor,
Even on the throne of his authority.

ANGIOLINA.
There seems to me enough in the conviction
Of a patrician guilty of a falsehood:
All other punishment were light unto
His loss of honor.

DOGE.
Such men have no honor,
They have but their vile lives—and these are spared.

ANGIOLINA.
You would not have him die for this offence?

Doge.

Not *now :*—being still alive, I'd have him live
Long as *he* can; he has ceased to merit death;
The guilty saved hath damn'd his hundred judges,
And he is pure, for now his crime is theirs.

Angiolina.

Oh! had this false and flippant libeller
Shed his young blood for his absurd lampoon,
Ne'er from that moment could this breast have known
A joyous hour, or dreamless slumber more.

Doge.

Does not the law of Heaven say blood for blood?
And he who *taints* kills more than he who sheds it.
Is it the *pain* of blows, or *shame* of blows,
That make such deadly to the sense of man?
Do not the laws of man say blood for honor?
And, less than honor, for a little gold?
Say not the laws of nations blood for treason?
Is't nothing to have fill'd these veins with poison
For their once healthful current? is it nothing
To have stain'd your name and mine—the noblest names?
Is't nothing to have brought into contempt
A prince before his people? to have fail'd
In the respect accorded by mankind
To youth in woman, and old age in man?
To virtue in your sex, and dignity
In ours?—But let them look to it who have saved him.

Angiolina.

Heaven bids us to forgive our enemies.

DOGE.
Doth Heaven forgive her own? Is Satan saved
From wrath eternal?

ANGIOLINA.
Do not speak thus wildly—
Heaven will alike forgive you and your foes.

DOGE.
Amen! May Heaven forgive them!

ANGIOLINA.
And will you?

DOGE.
Yes, when they are in heaven!

ANGIOLINA.
And not till then?

DOGE.
What matters my forgiveness? an old man's,
Worn out, scorn'd, spurn'd, abused; what matters then
My pardon more than my resentment, both
Being weak and worthless? I have lived too long.—
But let us change the argument.—My child!
My injured wife, the child of Loredano,
The brave, the chivalrous, how little deem'd
Thy father, wedding thee unto his friend,
That he was linking thee to shame!—Alas!
Shame without sin, for thou art faultless. Hadst thou
But had a different husband, *any* husband
In Venice save the Doge, this blight, this brand,
This blasphemy had never fallen upon thee.
So young, so beautiful, so good, so pure,
To suffer this, and yet be unavenged!

ANGIOLINA.

I am too well avenged, for you still love me,
And trust, and honor me; and all men know
That you are just, and I am true: what more
Could I require, or you command?

DOGE.

'Tis well,
And may be better; but whate'er betide,
Be thou at least kind to my memory.

ANGIOLINA.

Why speak you thus?

DOGE.

It is no matter why;
But I would still, whatever others think,
Have your respect both now and in my grave.

ANGIOLINA.

Why should you doubt it? has it ever fail'd?

DOGE.

Come hither, child; I would a word with you.
Your father was my friend; unequal fortune
Made him my debtor for some courtesies
Which bind the good more firmly: when, oppress'd
With his last malady, he will'd our union,
It was not to repay me, long repaid
Before by his great loyalty in friendship;
His object was to place your orphan beauty
In honorable safety from the perils,
Which, in this scorpion nest of vice, assail

A lonely and undower'd maid. I did not
Think with him, but would not oppose the thought
Which soothed his death-bed.

Angiolina.

I have not forgotten
The nobleness with which you bade me speak,
If my young heart held any preference
Which would have made me happier; nor your offer
To make my dowry equal to the rank
Of aught in Venice, and forego all claim
My father's last injunction gave you.

Doge.
        Thus,
'Twas not a foolish dotard's vile caprice,
Nor the false edge of aged appetite,
Which made me covetous of girlish beauty,
And a young bride: for in my fieriest youth
I sway'd such passions; nor was this my age
Infected with that leprosy of lust
Which taints the hoariest years of vicious men,
Making them ransack to the very last
The dregs of pleasure for their vanish'd joys;
Or buy in selfish marriage some young victim,
Too helpless to refuse a state that's honest,
Too feeling not to know herself a wretch.
Our wedlock was not of this sort; you had
Freedom from me to choose, and urged in answer
Your father's choice.

ANGIOLINA.

I did so; I would do so
In face of earth and heaven; for I have never
Repented for my sake; sometimes for yours,
In pondering o'er your late disquietudes.

DOGE.

I knew my heart would never treat you harshly;
I knew my days could not disturb you long;
And then the daughter of my earliest friend,
His worthy daughter, free to choose again,
Wealthier and wiser, in the ripest bloom
Of womanhood, more skilful to select
By passing these probationary years;
Inheriting a prince's name and riches,
Secured, by the short penance of enduring
An old man for some summers, against all
That law's chicane or envious kinsmen might
Have urged against her right; my best friend's child
Would choose more fitly in respect of years,
And not less truly in a faithful heart.

ANGIOLINA.

My lord, I look'd but to my father's wishes,
Hallow'd by his last words, and to my heart
For doing all its duties, and replying
With faith to him with whom I was affianced.
Ambitious hopes ne'er cross'd my dreams; and should
The hour you speak of come, it will be seen so.

DOGE.

I do believe you; and I know you true:
For love, romantic love, which in my youth

I knew to be illusion, and ne'er saw
Lasting, but often fatal, it had been
No lure for me, in my most passionate days,
And could not be so now, did such exist.
But such respect, and mildly paid regard
As a true feeling for your welfare, and
A free compliance with all honest wishes;
A kindness to your virtues, watchfulness
Not shown, but shadowing o'er such little failings
As youth is apt in, so as not to check
Rashly, but win you from them ere you knew
You had been won, but thought the change your choice;
A pride not in your beauty, but your conduct,—
A trust in you—a patriarchal love,
And not a doting homage—friendship, faith—
Such estimation in your eyes as these
Might claim, I hoped for.

     Angiolina.
And have ever had.

     Doge.
I think so. For the difference in our years,
You knew it, choosing me, and chose; I trusted
Not to my qualities, nor would have faith
In such, nor outward ornaments of nature,
Were I still in my five and twentieth spring;
I trusted to the blood of Loredano
Pure in your veins; I trusted to the soul
God gave you—to the truths your father taught you—
To your belief in heaven—to your mild virtues—
To your own faith and honor, for my own.

Angiolina.

You have done well.—I thank you for that trust,
Which I have never for one moment ceased
To honor you the more for.

Doge.

Where is honor,
Innate and precept-strengthen'd, 'tis the rock
Of faith connubial: where it is not—where
Light thoughts are lurking, or the vanities
Of worldly pleasure rankle in the heart,
Or sensual throbs convulse it, well I know
'Twere hopeless for humanity to dream
Of honesty in such infected blood,
Although 'twere wed to him it covets most:
An incarnation of the poet's god
In all his marble-chisell'd beauty, or
The demi-deity, Alcides, in
His majesty of superhuman manhood,
Would not suffice to bind where virtue is not;
It is consistency which forms and proves it:
Vice cannot fix, and virtue cannot change.
The once fall'n woman must forever fall;
For vice must have variety, while virtue
Stands like the sun, and all which rolls around
Drinks life, and light, and glory from her aspect.

Angiolina.

And seeing, feeling thus this truth in others,
(I pray you pardon me;) but wherefore yield you
To the most fierce of fatal passions, and

Disquiet your great thoughts with restless hate
Of such a thing as Steno?

Doge.

You mistake me.
It is not Steno who could move me thus;
Had it been so, he should——but let that pass.

Angiolina.

What is 't you feel so deeply, then, even now?

Doge.

The violated majesty of Venice,
At once insulted in her lord and laws.

Angiolina.

Alas! why will you thus consider it?

Doge.

I have thought on 't till——but let me lead you back
To what I urged; all these things being noted,
I wedded you; the world then did me justice
Upon the motive, and my conduct proved
They did me right, while yours was all to praise:
You had all freedom—all respect—all trust
From me and mine; and, born of those who made
Princes at home, and swept kings from their thrones
On foreign shores, in all things you appear'd
Worthy to be our first of native dames.

Angiolina.

To what does this conduct?

DOGE.

To thus much—that
A miscreant's angry breath may blast it all—
A villain, whom for his unbridled bearing,
Even in the midst of our great festival,
I caused to be conducted forth, and taught
How to demean himself in ducal chambers;
A wretch like this may leave upon the wall
The blighting venom of his sweltering heart,
And this shall spread itself in general poison;
And woman's innocence, man's honor, pass
Into a by-word; and the doubly felon
(Who first insulted virgin modesty
By a gross affront to your attendant damsels
Amidst the noblest of our dames in public)
Requite himself for his most just expulsion
By blackening publicly his sovereign's consort,
And be absolved by his upright compeers.

ANGIOLINA.

But he has been condemn'd into captivity.

DOGE.

For such as him a dungeon were acquittal;
And his brief term of mock-arrest will pass
Within a palace. But I've done with him;
The rest must be with you.

ANGIOLINA.

With me, my lord?

Doge.

Yes, Angiolina. Do not marvel: I
Have let this prey upon me till I feel
My life can not be long; and fain would have you
Regard the injunctions you will find within
This scroll (*Giving her a paper*)——Fear not; they
    are for your advantage:
Read them hereafter at the fitting hour.

Angiolina.

My lord, in life, and after life, you shall
Be honor'd still by me: but may your days
Be many yet——and happier than the present!
This passion will give way, and you will be
Serene, and what you should be—what you were.

Doge.

I will be what I should be, or be nothing!
But never more—oh! never, never more,
O'er the few days or hours which yet await
The blighted old age of Faliero, shall
Sweet Quiet shed her sunset! Never more
Those summer shadows rising from the past
Of a not ill-spent nor inglorious life,
Mellowing the last hours as the night approaches,
Shall soothe me to my moment of long rest.
I had but little more to task, or hope,
Save the regards due to the blood and sweat,
And the soul's labor through which I had toil'd
To make my country honor'd. As her servant—

Her servant, though her chief—I would have gone
Down to my fathers with a name serene
And pure as theirs; but this has been denied me.—
Would I had died at Zara!

ANGIOLINA.

There you saved
The state; then live to save her still. A day,
Another day like that would be the best
Reproof to them, and sole revenge for you.

DOGE.

But one such day occurs within an age,
My life is little less than one, and 'tis
Enough for Fortune to have granted *once*,
That which scarce one more favor'd citizen
May win in many states and years. But why
Thus speak I? Venice has forgot that day—
Then why should I remember it?—Farewell,
Sweet Angiolina! I must to my cabinet;
There's much for me to do—and the hour hastens.

ANGIOLINA.

Remember what you were.

DOGE.

It were in vain;
Joy's recollection is no longer joy,
While Sorrow's memory is a sorrow still.

ANGIOLINA.

At least, whate'er may urge, let me implore
That you will take some little pause of rest:

Your sleep for many nights has been so turbid,
That it had been relief to have awaked you,
Had I not hoped that Nature would o'erpower
At length the thoughts which shook your slumbers thus.
An hour of rest will give you to your toils
With fitter thoughts and freshen'd strength.

Doge.

I cannot—
I must not, if I could ; for never was
Such reason to be watchful : yet a few—
Yet a few days and dream-perturbed nights,
And I shall slumber well—but where ?—no matter.
Adieu, my Angiolina.

Angiolina.

Let me be
An instant—yet an instant your companion !
I cannot bear to leave you thus.

Doge.

Come then,
My gentle child—forgive me ; thou wert made
For better fortunes than to share in mine,
Now darkling in their close toward the deep vale
Where Death sits robed in his all-sweeping shadow.
When I am gone—it may be sooner than
Even these years warrant, for there is that stirring
Within—above—around, that in this city
Will make the cemeteries populous

As e'er they were by pestilence or war,—
When I *am* nothing, let that which I *was*
Be still sometimes a name on thy sweet lips,
A shadow in thy fancy, of a thing
Which would not have thee mourn it, but remember;—
Let us begone, my child—the time is pressing.

[*Exeunt.*

ANAH AND AHOLIBAMAH.

A woody and mountainous district near Mount Ararat.—Time, Midnight.

[*Enter* ANAH *and* AHOLIBAMAH.]

ANAH.
Our father sleeps; it is the hour when they
Who love us are accustom'd to descend
Through the deep clouds o'er rocky Ararat:—
How my heart beats!

AHOLIBAMAH.
    Let us proceed upon
Our invocation.

ANAH.
    But the stars are hidden.
I tremble.

AHOLIBAMAH.
So do I, but not with fear
Of aught save their delay.

ANAH.

My sister, though
I love Azaziel more than——oh, too much!
What was I going to say? my heart grows impious.

AHOLIBAMAH.

And where is the impiety of loving
Celestial natures?

ANAH.

But, Aholibamah,
I love our God less since his angel loved me:
This cannot be of good; and though I know not
That I do wrong, I feel a thousand fears
Which are not ominous of right.

AHOLIBAMAH.

Then wed thee
Unto some son of clay, and toil and spin!
There's Japhet loves thee well, hath loved thee long:
Marry, and bring forth dust?

ANAH.

I should have loved
Azaziel not less, were he mortal; yet
I am glad he is not. I can not outlive him.
And when I think that his immortal wings
Will one day hover o'er the sepulchre
Of the poor child of clay which so adored him,
As he adores the Highest, death becomes
Less terrible; but yet I pity him:

His grief will be of ages, or at least
Mine would be such for him, were I the Seraph,
And he the perishable.

    AHOLIBAMAH.
       Rather say,
That he will single forth some other daughter
Of Earth, and love her as he once loved Anah.

    ANAH.
And if it should be so, and she loved him,
Better thus than that he should weep for me.

    AHOLIBAMAH.
If I thought thus of Samiasa's love,
All Seraph as he is, I'd spurn him from me.
But to our invocation!—'Tis the hour.

    ANAH.
    Seraph!
   From thy sphere!
Whatever star contain thy glory;
 In the eternal depths of heaven
  Albeit thou watchest with "the seven,"
Though through space infinite and hoary
 Before thy bright wings worlds be driven,
   Yet hear!
Oh! think of her who holds thee dear!
 And though she nothing is to thee,
Yet think that thou art all to her.
  Thou canst not tell,—and never be
   Such pangs decreed to aught save me,—
    The bitterness of tears.

Eternity is in thine years,
Unborn, undying beauty in thine eyes;
With me thou canst not sympathize,
 Except in love, and there thou must
 Acknowledge that more loving dust
Ne'er wept beneath the skies.
Thou walk'st thy many worlds, thou see'st
 The face of him who made thee great,
As he hath made me of the least
 Of those cast out from Eden's gate:
  Yet, Seraph dear!
  Oh hear!
For thou hast loved me, and I would not die
 Until I know what I must die in knowing,
That thou forget'st in thine eternity
 Her whose heart death could not keep from o'erflowing
For thee, immortal essence as thou art!
Great is their love who love in sin and fear;
And such, I feel, are waging in my heart
 A war unworthy: to an Adamite
Forgive, my Seraph! that such thoughts appear,
 For sorrow is our element;
  Delight
 An Eden kept afar from sight,
 Though sometimes with our visions blent.
  The hour is near
Which tells me we are not abandon'd quite.—
  Appear! Appear!
  Seraph!
 My own Azaziel! be but here,
And leave the stars to their own light.

AHOLIBAMAH.

Samiasa!
  Wheresoe'er
Thou rulest in the upper air—
Or warring with the spirits who may dare
  Dispute with Him
Who made all empires, empire; or recalling
Some wandering star, which shoots through the abyss,
  Whose tenants dying, while their world is falling,
Share the dim destiny of clay in this,
  Or joining with the inferior cherubim,
  Thou deignest to partake their hymn—
      Samiasa!
  I call thee, I await thee, and I love thee.
  Many may worship thee, that will I not:
  If that thy spirit down to mine may move thee,
    Descend and share my lot!
    Though I be form'd of clay,
      And thou of beams
    More bright than those of day
      On Eden's streams,
Thine immortality can not repay
  With love more warm than mine
My love. There is a ray
  In me, which, though forbidden yet to shine,
  I feel was lighted at thy God's and thine.
It may be hidden long: death and decay
  Our mother Eve bequeath'd us—but my heart
Defies it: though this life must pass away,
  Is *that* a cause for thee and me to part?
Thou art immortal—so am I: I feel—

I feel my immortality o'ersweep
All pains, all tears, all time, all fears, and peal,
   Like the eternal thunders of the deep,
Into my ears this truth—" Thou liv'st forever!"
      But if it be in joy
    I know not, nor would know;
That secret rests with the Almighty giver
   Who folds in clouds the founts of bliss and wo.
     But thee and me he never can destroy;
Change us he may, but not o'erwhelm; we are
Of as eternal essence, and must war
With him if he will war with us: with *thee*
   I can share all things, even immortal sorrow;
For thou hast ventured to share life with *me*,
And shall *I* shrink from thine eternity?
   No! though the serpent's sting should pierce me thorough,
And thou thyself wert like the serpent, coil
Around me still! and I will smile,
    And curse thee not; but hold
    Thee in as warm a fold
    As——but descend, and prove
    A mortal's love
For an immortal. If the skies contain
More joy than thou canst give and take, remain!

ANAH.

Sister! sister! I view them winging
Their bright way through the parted night.

AHOLIBAMAH.

The clouds from off their pinions flinging,
As though they bore to-morrow's light.

ANAH.
But if our father see the sight!

AHOLIBAMAH.
He would but deem it was the moon
Rising unto some sorcerer's tune
An hour too soon.

ANAH.
They come! *he* comes!—Azaziel!

AHOLIBAMAH.
Haste
To meet them! Oh! for wings to bear
My spirit, while they hover there,
To Samiasa's breast!

ANAH.
Lo! they have kindled all the west,
Like a returning sunset;—lo!
On Ararat's late secret crest
A mild and many-color'd bow,
The remnant of their flashing path,
Now shines! and now behold! it hath
Return'd to night, as rippling foam,
Which the leviathan hath lash'd
From his unfathomable home,
When sporting on the face of the calm deep,
Subsides soon after he again hath dash'd
Down, down, to where the ocean's fountains sleep.

AHOLIBAMAH.

They have touch'd earth! Samiasa!

ANAH.

My Azaziel!

MYRRHA.

Enter SARDANAPALUS *effeminately dressed, his Head crowned with Flowers, and his Robe negligently flowing, attended by a Train of Women and young Slaves, among them* MYRRHA.

SARDANAPALUS, (*speaking to some of his attendants.*)
LET the pavilion over the Euphrates
Be garlanded, and lit, and furnish'd forth
For an especial banquet; at the hour
Of midnight we will sup there: see naught wanting,
And bid the galley be prepared. There is
A cooling breeze which crisps the broad clear river:
We will embark anon. Fair nymphs, who deign
To share the soft hours of Sardanapalus,
We'll meet again in that the sweetest hour,
When we shall gather like the stars above us,
And you will form a heaven as bright as theirs;
Till then, let each be mistress of her time,
And thou, my own Ionian Myrrha, choose,
Wilt thou along with them or me?

Myrrha.

My lord——

Sardanapalus.

My lord, my life! why answerest thou so coldly?
It is the curse of kings to be so answer'd.
Rule thy own hours, thou rulest mine—say, wouldst thou
Accompany our guests, or charm away
The moments from me?

Myrrha.

The king's choice is mine.

Sardanapalus.

I pray thee say not so: my chiefest joy
Is to contribute to thine every wish.
I do not dare to breathe my own desire,
Lest it should clash with thine; for thou art still
Too prompt to sacrifice thy thoughts for others.

Myrrha.

I would remain: I have no happiness
Save in beholding thine; yet——

Sardanapalus.

Yet! what YET?
Thy own sweet will shall be the only barrier
Which ever rises betwixt thee and me.

Myrrha.

I think the present is the wonted hour
Of council; it were better I retire.

SALEMENES, (*coming forward.*)
The Ionian slave says well: let her retire.

SARDANAPALUS.
Who answers? How now, brother?

SALEMENES.
The *queen's* brother,
And your most faithful vassal, royal lord.
*   *   *   *   *   *

SARDANAPALUS.
Slave, tell
The Ionian Myrrha we would crave her presence.

ATTENDANT.
King, she is here.

[MYRRHA *enters.*]

SARDANAPALUS.
(*Apart to Attendant.*) Away!
(*Addressing* MYRRHA.) Beautiful being!
Thou dost almost anticipate my heart;
It throbb'd for thee, and here thou comest: let me
Deem that some unknown influence, some sweet oracle,
Communicates between us, though unseen,
In absence, and attracts us to each other.

MYRRHA.
There doth.

SARDANAPALUS.
I know there doth, but not its name:
What is it?

Myrrha.

In my native land a God,
And in my heart a feeling like a God's,
Exalted; yet I own 'tis only mortal;
For what I feel is humble, and yet happy—
That is, it would be happy; but—— [Myrrha *pauses.*

Sardanapalus.

There comes
Forever something between us and what
We deem our happiness: let me remove
The barrier which that hesitating accent
Proclaims to thine, and mine is seal'd.

Myrrha.

My lord!—

Sardanapalus.

My lord—my king—sire—sovereign! thus it is—
Forever thus, address'd with awe. I ne'er
Can see a smile, unless in some broad banquet's
Intoxicating glare, when the buffoons
Have gorged themselves up to equality,
Or I have quaff'd me down to their abasement.
Myrrha, I can hear all these things, these names,
Lord—king—sire—monarch—nay, time was, I prized
    them;
That is, I suffer'd them—from slaves and nobles;
But when they falter from the lips I love,
The lips which have been press'd to mine, a chill
Comes o'er my heart, a cold sense of the falsehood
Of this my station, which represses feeling

In those for whom I have felt most, and makes me
Wish that I could lay down the dull tiara,
And share a cottage on the Caucasus
With thee, and wear no crowns but those of flowers.

>   MYRRHA.
> Would that we could!

>   SARDANAPALUS.
> And dost *thou* feel this?—Why?

>   MYRRHA.
> Then thou wouldst know what thou canst never know.

>   SARDANAPALUS.
> And that is——

>   MYRRHA.
> The true value of a heart;
> At least, a woman's.

>   SARDANAPALUS.
> I have proved a thousand—
> A thousand, and a thousand.

>   MYRRHA.
> Hearts?

>   SARDANAPALUS.
> I think so.

>   MYRRHA.
> Not one! the time may come thou mayst.

>   SARDANAPALUS.
> It will.

Hear, Myrrha; Salemenes has declared—
Or why or how he hath divined it, Belus,
Who founded our great realm, knows more than I—
But Salemenes hath declared my throne
In peril.

MYRRHA.

He did well.

SARDANAPALUS.

And say'st *thou* so?
Thou whom he spurn'd so harshly, and now dared
Drive from our presence with his savage jeers,
And made thee weep and blush?

MYRRHA.

I should do both
More frequently, and he did well to call me
Back to my duty. But thou spak'st of peril—
Peril to thee——

SARDANAPALUS.

Ay, from dark plots and snares
From Medes—and discontented troops and nations.
I know not what—a labyrinth of things—
A maze of mutter'd threats and mysteries:
Thou know'st the man—it is his usual custom.
But he is honest. Come, we'll think no more on't—
But of the midnight festival.

MYRRHA.

'Tis time
To think of aught save festivals. Thou hast not
Spurn'd his sage cautions?

SARDANAPALUS.
What?—and dost thou fear?

MYRRHA.
Fear!—I'm a Greek, and how should I fear death?
A slave, and wherefore should I dread my freedom?

SARDANAPALUS.
Then wherefore dost thou turn so pale?

MYRRHA.
I love.

SARDANAPALUS.
And do not I? I love thee far—far more
Than either the brief life or the wide realm,
Which, it may be, are menaced;—yet I blench not.

MYRRHA.
That means thou lovest not thyself nor me;
For he who loves another loves himself,
Even for that other's sake. This is too rash:
Kingdoms and lives are not to be so lost.

SARDANAPALUS.
Lost!—why, who is the aspiring chief who dared
Assume to win them?

MYRRHA.
Who is he should dread
To try so much? When he who is their ruler
Forgets himself, will they remember him?

SARDANAPALUS.
Myrrha!
17

MYRRHA.

Frown not upon me: you have smiled
Too often on me not to make those frowns
Bitterer to bear than any punishment
Which they may augur.—King, I am your subject!
Master, I am your slave! Man, I have loved you!—
Loved you, I know not by what fatal weakness,
Although a Greek, and born a foe to monarchs—
A slave, and hating fetters—an Ionian,
And, therefore, when I love a stranger, more
Degraded by that passion than by chains!
Still I have loved you. If that love were strong
Enough to overcome all former nature,
Shall it not claim the privilege to save you?

SARDANAPALUS.

Save me, my beauty! Thou art very fair,
And what I seek of thee is love—not safety.

MYRRHA.

And without love where dwells security?

SARDANAPALUS.

I speak of woman's love.

MYRRHA.

The very first
Of human life must spring from woman's breast,
Your first small words are taught you from her lips,
Your first tears quench'd by her, and your last sighs
Too often breathed out in a woman's hearing,
When men have shrunk from the ignoble care
Of watching the last hour of him who led them.

SARDANAPALUS.

My eloquent Ionian! thou speak'st music,
The very chorus of the tragic song
I have heard thee talk of as the favorite pastime
Of thy far father-land. Nay, weep not—calm thee.

MYRRHA.

I weep not.—But I pray thee, do not speak
About my fathers or their land.

SARDANAPALUS.

Yet oft
Thou speakest of them.

MYRRHA.

True—true: constant thought
Will overflow in words unconsciously;
But when another speaks of Greece, it wounds me.

SARDANAPALUS.

Well, then, how wouldst thou *save* me, as thou saidst?

MYRRHA.

By teaching thee to save thyself, and not
Thyself alone, but these vast realms, from all
The rage of the worst war—the war of brethren!

SARDANAPALUS.

Why, child, I loathe all war, and warriors;
I live in peace and pleasure: what can man
Do more?

Myrrha.

Alas! my lord, with common men
There needs too oft the show of war to keep
The substance of sweet peace; and for a king,
'Tis sometimes better to be fear'd than loved.

Sardanapalus.

And I have never sought but for the last.

Myrrha.

And now art neither.

Sardanapalus.

Dost *thou* say so, Myrrha?

Myrrha.

I speak of civic popular love, *self*-love,
Which means that men are kept in awe and law,
Yet not oppress'd—at least they must not think so;
Or if they think so, deem it necessary,
To ward off worse oppression, their own passions.
A king of feasts, and flowers, and wine, and revel,
And love, and mirth, was never king of glory.

Sardanapalus.

Glory! what's that?

Myrrha.

Ask of the gods thy fathers.

Sardanapalus.

They cannot answer; when the priests speak for them,
'Tis for some small addition to the temple.

MYRRHA.
Look to the annals of thine empire's founders.

SARDANAPALUS.
They are so blotted o'er with blood, I cannot.
But what wouldst have? the empire *has been* founded.
I cannot go on multiplying empires.

MYRRHA.
Preserve thine own.

SARDANAPALUS.
At least, I will enjoy it.
Come, Myrrha, let us go on to the Euphrates:
The hour invites, the galley is prepared,
And the pavilion, deck'd for our return,
In fit adornment for the evening banquet,
Shall blaze with beauty and with light, until
It seems unto the stars which are above us
Itself an opposite star; and we will sit
Crown'd with fresh flowers like——

MYRRHA.
Victims.

SARDANAPALUS.
No, like sovereigns,
The shepherd kings of patriarchal times,
Who knew no brighter gems than summer wreaths,
And none but tearless triumphs. Let us on.

* * * * *

[SARDANAPALUS *discovered sleeping upon a Couch, and occasionally disturbed in his Slumbers, with* MYRRHA *watching.*]

MYRRHA, (*sola, gazing.*)
I have stolen upon his rest, if rest it be,
Which thus convulses slumber: shall I wake him?
No, he seems calmer. Oh, thou God of Quiet!
Whose reign is o'er seal'd eyelids and soft dreams,
Or deep, deep sleep, so as to be unfathom'd,
Look like thy brother, Death—so still—so stirless—
For then we are happiest, as it may be, we
Are happiest of all within the realm
Of thy stern, silent, and unwakening twin.
Again he moves—again the play of pain
Shoots o'er his features, as the sudden gust
Crisps the reluctant lake that lay so calm
Beneath the mountain shadow; or the blast
Ruffles the autumn leaves, that drooping cling
Faintly and motionless to their loved boughs.
I must awake him—yet not yet: who knows
From what I rouse him? It seems pain; but if
I quicken him to heavier pain? The fever
Of this tumultuous night, the grief too of
His wound, though slight, may cause all this, and shake
Me more to see than him to suffer. No:
Let Nature use her own maternal means,—
And I await to second, not disturb her.

* * * * * *

MYRRHA.
And dost thou think
A Greek girl dare not do for love, that which
An Indian widow braves for custom?

SARDANAPALUS.
Then
We but await the signal.

MYRRHA.
It is long
In sounding.

SARDANAPALUS.
Now, farewell; one last embrace.

MYRRHA.
Embrace, but *not* the last; there is one more.

SARDANAPALUS.
True, the commingling fire will mix our ashes.

MYRRHA.
And pure as is my love to thee, shall they,
Purged from the dross of earth, and earthly passion,
Mix pale with thine. A single thought yet irks me.

SARDANAPALUS.
Say it.

MYRRHA.
It is that no kind hand will gather
The dust of both into one urn.

SARDANAPALUS.
The better:
Rather let them be borne abroad upon
The winds of heaven, and scatter'd into air,
Than be polluted more by human hands
Of slaves and traitors.

MYRRHA.

Then farewell, thou earth!
And loveliest spot of earth! farewell, Ionia!
Be thou still free and beautiful, and far
Aloof from desolation! My last prayer
Was for thee, my last thoughts, save *one*, were of thee!

SARDANAPALUS.

And that?

MYRRHA.

Is yours.

[*The trumpet of* PANIA *sounds without.*

SARDANAPALUS.

Hark!

MYRRHA.

Now!

SARDANAPALUS.

Adieu, Assyria!
I loved thee well, my own, my fathers' land,
And better as my country than my kingdom.

[*He mounts the pile.*

Now, Myrrha!

MYRRHA.

Art thou ready?

SARDANAPALUS.

As the torch in thy grasp. [MYRRHA *fires the pile.*

MYRRHA.

'Tis fired! I come.

[*As* MYRRHA *springs forward to throw herself into the flames, the Curtain falls.*

OLIMPIA.

[*Enter* OLIMPIA, *flying from the pursuit—She springs upon the Altar.*]

SOLDIER.
She's mine!

ANOTHER SOLDIER, (*opposing the former.*)
You lie, I track'd her first; and were she
The Pope's niece, I'll not yield her.   [*They fight.*

THIRD SOLDIER, (*advancing towards* OLIMPIA.)
You may settle
Your claims; I'll make mine good.

OLIMPIA.
Infernal slave!
You touch me not alive.

THIRD SOLDIER.
Alive or dead!

OLIMPIA, (*embracing a massive crucifix.*)
Respect your God!

THIRD SOLDIER.

Yes, when he shines in gold.
Girl, you but grasp your dowry.

[*As he advances,* OLIMPIA, *with a strong and sudden effort,
casts down the crucifix: it strikes the Soldier, who falls.*

THIRD SOLDIER.

Oh, great God!

OLIMPIA.

Ah! now you recognize him.

THIRD SOLDIER.

My brain's crush'd!
Comrades, help, ho! All's darkness! [*He dies.*

OTHER SOLDIERS, (*coming up.*)

Slay her, although she had a thousand lives:
She hath kill'd our comrade.

OLIMPIA.

Welcome such a death!
You have no life to give, which the worst slave
Would take. Great God! through thy redeeming Son,
And thy Son's Mother, now receive me as
I would approach thee, worthy her, and him, and thee!

[*Enter* ARNOLD.]

ARNOLD.

What do I see? Accursed jackals!
Forbear!

CÆSAR, (*aside and laughing.*)
Ha! ha! here's equity! The dogs
Have as much right as he. But to the issue!

SOLDIERS.
Count, she hath slain our comrade.

ARNOLD.
With what weapon?

SOLDIERS.
The cross, beneath which he is crush'd; behold him
Lie there, more like a worm than man; she cast it
Upon his head.

ARNOLD.
Even so; there is a woman
Worthy a brave man's liking. Were ye such,
Ye would have honor'd her. But get ye hence,
And thank your meanness, other God you have none,
For your existence. Had you touch'd a hair
Of those dishevell'd locks, I would have thinn'd
Your ranks more than the enemy. Away!
Ye jackals! gnaw the bones the lion leaves,
But not even these till he permits.

A SOLDIER, (*murmuring.*)
The lion
Might conquer for himself then.

ARNOLD, (*cuts him down.*)
Mutineer!
Rebel in hell—you shall obey on earth!
[*The soldiers assault* ARNOLD.

Come on! I'm glad on't! I will show you, slaves,
How you should be commanded, and who led you
First o'er the wall you were so shy to scale,
Until I waved my banners from its height,
As you are bold within it.
    [ARNOLD *moves down the foremost; the rest throw*
      down their arms.

SOLDIERS.

Mercy! mercy!

ARNOLD.

Then learn to grant it. Have I taught you *who*
Led you o'er Rome's eternal battlements?

SOLDIERS.

We saw it, and we know it; yet forgive
A moment's error in the heat of conquest—
The conquest which you led to.

ARNOLD.

Get you hence!
Hence to your quarters! you will find them fix'd
In the Colonna palace.

OLIMPIA, (*aside.*)
    In my father's
House!

ARNOLD, (*to the soldiers.*)
Leave your arms; ye have no further need
Of such: the city's rendered. And mark well
You keep your hands clean, or I'll find out a stream
As red as Tiber now runs, for your baptism.

SOLDIERS, (*deposing their arms and departing.*)
We obey!

ARNOLD, (*to* OLIMPIA.)
Lady, you are safe.

OLIMPIA.

I should be so,
Had I a knife even; but it matters not—
Death hath a thousand gates; and on the marble,
Even at the altar foot, whence I look down
Upon destruction, shall my head be dash'd,
Ere thou ascend it. God forgive thee, man!

ARNOLD.

I wish to merit his forgiveness, and
Thine own, although I have not injured thee.

OLIMPIA.

No! Thou hast only sack'd my native land,—
No injury!—and made my father's house
A den of thieves! No injury!—this temple—
Slippery with Roman and with holy gore.
No injury! And now thou wouldst preserve me,
To be——but that shall never be!

[*She raises her eyes to Heaven, folds her robe round her, and prepares to dash herself down on the side of the Altar opposite to that where* ARNOLD *stands.*

ARNOLD.
Hold! hold!
I swear.

OLIMPIA.

Spare thine already forfeit soul
A perjury for which even hell would loathe thee.
I know thee.

ARNOLD.

No, thou know'st me not; I am not
Of these men, though——

OLIMPIA.

I judge thee by thy mates;
It is for God to judge thee as thou art.
I see thee purple with the blood of Rome;
Take mine, 'tis all thou e'er shalt have of me,
And here, upon the marble of this temple,
Where the baptismal font baptized me God's,
I offer him a blood less holy
But not less pure (pure as it left me then,
A redeem'd infant) than the holy water
The saints have sanctified!

[OLIMPIA *waves her hand to* ARNOLD *with disdain, and dashes herself on the pavement from the Altar.*

ADAH.

The Earth near the Garden of Eden.

[*Enter* CAIN *and* ADAH.]

ADAH.
Hush! tread softly, Cain.

CAIN.
I will; but wherefore?

ADAH.
Our little Enoch sleeps upon yon bed
Of leaves, beneath the cypress.

CAIN.
Cypress! 'tis
A gloomy tree, which looks as if it mourn'd
O'er what it shadows; wherefore didst thou choose it
For our child's canopy?

ADAH.

Because its branches
Shut out the sun like night, and therefore seem
Fitting to shadow slumber.

CAIN.

Ay, the last—
And longest; but no matter—lead me to him.
[*They go up to the child.*
How lovely he appears! his little cheeks,
In their pure incarnation, vying with
The rose leaves strewn beneath them.

ADAH.

And his lips, too,
How beautifully parted! No; you shall not
Kiss him, at least not now: he will awake soon—
His hour of mid-day rest is nearly over;
But it were a pity to disturb him till
'Tis closed.

CAIN.

You have said well; I will contain
My heart till then. He smiles, and sleeps!—Sleep on,
And smile, thou little, young inheritor
Of a world scarce less young: sleep on, and smile!
Thine are the hours and days when both are cheering
And innocent! *thou* hast not pluck'd the fruit—
Thou know'st not thou art naked! Must the time
Come thou shalt be amerced for sins unknown,
Which were not mine nor thine? But now sleep on!
His cheeks are reddening into deeper smiles,

And shining lids are trembling o'er his long
Lashes, dark as the cypress which waves o'er them ;
Half open, from beneath them the clear blue
Laughs out, although in slumber. He must dream—
Of what? Of Paradise!—Ay! dream of it,
My disinherited boy! 'Tis but a dream ;
For never more thyself, thy sons, nor fathers,
Shall walk in that forbidden place of joy!

ADAH.

Dear Cain! Nay, do not whisper o'er our son
Such melancholy yearnings o'er the past :
Why wilt thou always mourn for Paradise?
Can we not make another?

CAIN.

Where?

ADAH.

Here, or
Where'er thou wilt : where'er thou art, I feel not
The want of this so much regretted Eden.
Have I not thee, our boy, our sire, and brother,
And Zillah—our sweet sister, and our Eve,
To whom we owe so much besides our birth?

CAIN.

Yes—death, too, is among the debts we owe her.

ADAH.

Cain! that proud spirit who withdrew thee hence,
Hath sadden'd thine still deeper. I had hoped
The promised wonders which thou hast beheld,

Visions, thou say'st, of past and present worlds,
Would have composed thy mind into the calm
Of a contented knowledge; but I see
Thy guide hath done thee evil: still I thank him,
And can forgive him all, that he so soon
Hath given thee back to us.

CAIN.

So soon?

ADAH.

'Tis scarcely
Two hours since ye departed: two *long* hours
To *me*, but only *hours* upon the sun.

CAIN.

And yet I have approach'd that sun, and seen
Worlds which he once shone on, and never more
Shall light; and worlds he never lit: methought
Years had roll'd o'er my absence.

ADAH.

Hardly hours.

CAIN.

The mind then hath capacity of time,
And measures it by that which it beholds,
Pleasing or painful; little or almighty.
I had beheld the immemorial works
Of endless beings; skirr'd extinguish'd worlds;
And, gazing on eternity, methought
I had borrow'd more by a few drops of ages
From its immensity; but now I feel
My littleness again. Well said the spirit,
That I was nothing!

ADAH.
Wherefore said he so?
Jehovah said not that.

CAIN.
No: *he* contents him
With making us the *nothing* which we are;
And after flattering dust with glimpses of
Eden and Immortality, resolves
It back to dust again—for what?

ADAH.
Thou know'st—
Even for our parents' error.

CAIN.
What is that
To us? they sinn'd, then *let them* die!

ADAH.
Thou hast not spoken well, nor is that thought
Thy own, but of the spirit who was with thee.
Would *I* could die for them, so *they* might live!

CAIN.
Why, so say I—provided that one victim
Might satiate the insatiable of life,
And that our little rosy sleeper there
Might never taste of death nor human sorrow,
Nor hand it down to those who spring from him.

ADAH.
How know we that some such atonement one day
May not redeem our race?

CAIN.

By sacrificing
The harmless for the guilty? what atonement
Were there? why, *we* are innocent: what have we
Done, that we must be victims for a deed
Before our birth, or need have victims to
Atone for this mysterious, nameless sin—
If it be such a sin to seek for knowledge?

ADAH.

Alas! thou sinnest now, my Cain: thy words
Sound impious in mine ears.

CAIN.

Then leave me!

ADAH.

Never,
Though thy God left thee.

CAIN.

Say, what have we here?

ADAH.

The fruits of the earth, the early, beautiful
Blossom and bud, and bloom of flowers and fruits.
These are a goodly offering to the Lord,
Given with a gentle and a contrite spirit.

CAIN.

I have toil'd, and till'd, and sweaten in the sun
According to the curse!—must I do more?
For what should I be gentle? for a war
With all the elements ere they will yield

The bread we eat? For what must I be grateful?
For being dust, and grovelling in the dust,
Till I return to dust? If I am nothing—
For nothing shall I be an hypocrite,
And seem well-pleased with pain? For what should I
Be contrite? for my father's sin, already
Expiate with what we all have undergone,
And to be more than expiated by
The ages prophesied, upon our seed.
Little deems our young blooming sleeper, there,
The germs of an eternal misery
To myriads is within him! better 'twere
I snatch'd him in his sleep, and dash'd him 'gainst
The rocks, than let him live to——

ADAH.

Oh, my God!
Touch not the child—my child! *thy* child! Oh Cain!

CAIN.

Fear not! for all the stars, and all the power
Which sways them, I would not accost yon infant
With ruder greeting than a father's kiss.

ADAH.

Then, why so awful in thy speech?

CAIN.

I said,
'Twere better that he ceased to live, than give
Life to so much of sorrow as he must
Endure, and, harder still, bequeath; but since

That saying jars you, let us only say—
'Twere better that he never had been born.

ADAH.

Oh, do not say so! Where were then the joys,
The mother's joys of watching, nourishing,
And loving him? Soft! he awakes. Sweet Enoch!
[*She goes to the child.*

Oh Cain! look on him; see how full of life,
Of strength, of bloom, of beauty, and of joy,
How like to me—how like to thee, when gentle,
For *then* we are *all* alike; is't not so, Cain?
Mother, and sire, and son, our features are
Reflected in each other; as they are
In the clear waters, when *they* are *gentle*, and
When *thou* art *gentle*. Love us, then, my Cain!
And love thyself for our sakes, for we love thee.
Look! how he laughs and stretches out his arms,
And opens wide his blue eyes upon thine,
To hail his father; while his little form
Flutters as wing'd with joy. Talk not of pain!
The childless cherubs well might envy thee
The pleasures of a parent! Bless him, Cain!
As yet he hath no words to thank thee, but
His heart will, and thine own too.

CAIN.

Bless thee, boy!
If that a mortal blessing may avail thee,
To save thee from the serpent's curse!

ADAH.

It shall.

DONNA INEZ.

———— A LEARNED lady, famed
    For every branch of every science known—
In every Christian language ever named,
    With virtues equall'd by her wit alone,
She made the cleverest people quite ashamed,
    And even the good with inward envy groan,
Finding themselves so very much exceeded
In their own way by all the things that she did.

Her memory was a mine: she knew by heart
    All Calderon and greater part of Lopé,
So that if any actor miss'd his part
    She could have served him for the prompter's copy;
For her Feinagle's were a useless art,
    And he himself obliged to shut up shop—he
Could never make a memory so fine as
That which adorn'd the brain of Donna Inez.

Her favorite science was the mathematical,
    Her noblest virtue was her magnanimity,
Her wit (she sometimes tried at wit) was Attic all,
    Her serious sayings darken'd to sublimity;
In short, in all things she was fairly what I call
    A prodigy—her morning dress was dimity,
Her evening silk, or, in the summer, muslin,
And other stuffs, with which I won't stay puzzling.

Some women use their tongues—she *look'd* a lecture,
    Each eye a sermon, and her brow a homily,
An all-in-all sufficient self-director,
    Like the lamented late Sir Samuel Romilly,
The Law's expounder, and the State's corrector,
    Whose suicide was almost an anomaly—
One sad example more, that "All is vanity,"—
(The jury brought their verdict in "Insanity.")

In short, she was a walking calculation,
    Miss Edgeworth's novels stepping from their covers,
Or Mrs. Trimmer's books on education,
    Or "Cœlebs' Wife" set out in quest of lovers,
Morality's prim personification,
    In which not Envy's self a flaw discovers;
To others' share let "female errors fall,"
For she had not even one—the worst of all.

Oh! she was perfect past all parallel—
    Of any modern female saint's comparison;
So far above the cunning powers of hell,
    Her guardian angel had given up his garrison

Even her minutest motions went as well
    As those of the best time-piece made by Harrison:
In virtues nothing earthly could surpass her,
    Save thine "incomparable oil," Macassar!

Now Donna Inez had, with all her merit,
    A great opinion of her own good qualities;
Neglect, indeed, requires a saint to bear it,
    And such, indeed, she was in her moralities;
But then she had a devil of a spirit,
    And sometimes mix'd up fancies with realities,
And let few opportunities escape
Of getting her liege lord into a scrape.

This was an easy matter with a man
    Oft in the wrong, and never on his guard;
And even the wisest, do the best they can,
    Have moments, hours, and days, so unprepared,
That you might "brain them with their lady's fan;"
    And sometimes ladies hit exceeding hard,
And fans turn into falchions in fair hands,
And why and wherefore no one understands.

Don Jóse and the Donna Inez led
    For some time an unhappy sort of life,
Wishing each other, not divorced, but dead;
    They lived respectably as man and wife,
Their conduct was exceedingly well-bred,
    And gave no outward signs of inward strife,
Until at length the smother'd fire broke out,
And put the business past all kind of doubt.

For Inez call'd some druggists, and physicians,
    And tried to prove her loving lord was *mad*,
But as he had some lucid intermissions,
    She next decided he was only *bad*;
Yet when they ask'd her for her depositions,
    No sort of explanation could be had,
Save that her duty both to man and God
Required this conduct—which seem'd very odd.

She kept a journal, where his faults were noted,
    And open'd certain trunks of books and letters,
All which might, if occasion served, be quoted;
    And then she had all Seville for abettors,
Besides her good old grandmother, (who doted;)
    The hearers of her case became repeaters,
Then advocates, inquisitors, and judges,
Some for amusement, others for old grudges.

And then this best and meekest woman bore
    With such serenity her husband's woes,
Just as the Spartan ladies did of yore,
    Who saw their spouses kill'd, and nobly chose
Never to say a word about them more—
    Calmly she heard each calumny that rose,
And saw *his* agonies with such sublimity,
That all the world exclaim'd, "What magnanimity!"

DONNA JULIA.

The darkness of her Oriental eye
   Accorded with her Moorish origin;
(Her blood was not all Spanish, by the by;
   In Spain, you know, this is a sort of sin.)
When proud Granada fell, and, forced to fly,
   Boabdil wept, of Donna Julia's kin
Some went to Africa, some stay'd in Spain,
Her great great grandmamma chose to remain.

Her eye (I'm very fond of handsome eyes)
   Was large and dark, suppressing half its fire
Until she spoke, then through its soft disguise
   Flash'd an expression more of pride than ire,
And love than either; and there would arise
   A something in them which was not desire,
But would have been, perhaps, but for the soul
Which struggled through and chasten'd down the whole.

Her glossy hair was cluster'd o'er a brow
  Bright with intelligence, and fair, and smooth;
Her eyebrow's shape was like the aërial bow,
  Her cheek all purple with the beam of youth,
Mounting, at times, to a transparent glow,
  As if her veins ran lightning; she, in sooth,
Possess'd an air and grace by no means common:
Her stature tall—I hate a dumpy woman.

Juan she saw, and, as a pretty child,
  Caress'd him often—such a thing might be
Quite innocently done, and harmless styled,
  When she had twenty years, and thirteen he;
But I am not so sure I should have smiled
  When he was sixteen, Julia twenty-three;
These few short years make wondrous alterations,
Particularly amongst sunburnt nations.

Whate'er the cause might be, they had become
  Changed; for the dame grew distant, the youth shy,
Their looks cast down, their greetings almost dumb,
  And much embarrassment in either eye:
There surely will be little doubt with some
  That Donna Julia knew the reason why,
But as for Juan, he had no more notion
Than he who never saw the sea of ocean.

Yet Julia's very coldness still was kind,
  And tremulously gentle her small hand
Withdrew itself from his, but left behind
  A little pressure, thrilling, and so bland

And slight, so very slight, that to the mind
    'Twas but a doubt; but ne'er magician's wand
Wrought change with all Armida's fairy art
Like what this light touch left on Juan's heart.

And if she met him, though she smiled no more,
    She look'd a sadness sweeter than her smile,
As if her heart had deeper thoughts in store
    She must not own, but cherish'd more the while
For that compression in its burning core;
    Even innocence itself has many a wile,
And will not dare to trust itself with truth,
And love is taught hypocrisy from youth.

But passion most dissembles, yet betrays
    Even by its darkness; as the blackest sky
Foretells the heaviest tempest, it displays
    Its workings through the vainly guarded eye,
And in whatever aspect it arrays
    Itself, 'tis still the same hypocrisy;
Coldness or anger, even disdain or hate,
Are masks it often wears, and still too late.

Then there were sighs, the deeper for suppression,
    And stolen glances sweeter for the theft,
And burning blushes, though for no transgression,
    Tremblings when met, and restlessness when left;
All these are little preludes to possession,
    Of which young passion cannot be bereft,
And merely tend to show how greatly love is
Embarrass'd at first starting with a novice.

How beautiful she look'd! her conscious heart
   Glow'd in her cheek, and yet she felt no wrong.
Oh Love! how perfect in thy mystic art,
   Strengthening the weak, and trampling on the strong.
How self-deceitful is the sagest part
   Of mortals whom thy lure hath led along—
The precipice she stood on was immense,
So was her creed in her own innocence.

HAIDÉE

Her brow was overhung with coins of gold,
    That sparkled o'er the auburn of her hair,
Her clustering hair, whose longer locks were roll'd
    In braids behind; and though her stature were
Even of the highest for a female mould,
    They nearly reach'd her heel; and in her air
There was a something which bespoke command,
As one who was a lady in the land.

Her hair, I said, was auburn; but her eyes
    Were black as death, their lashes the same hue,
Of downcast length, in whose silk shadow lies
    Deepest attraction; for when to the view
Forth from its raven fringe the full glance flies,
    Ne'er with such force the swiftest arrow flew;
'Tis as the snake late coil'd, who pours his length,
And hurls at once his venom and his strength.

Her brow was white and low, her cheek's pure dye
    Like twilight rosy still with the set sun;
Short upper lip—sweet lips! that make us sigh
    Ever to have seen such; for she was one
Fit for the model of a statuary,
    (A race of mere impostors, when all's done—
I've seen much finer women, ripe and real,
Than all the nonsense of their stone ideal.)

And such was she, the lady of the cave:
    Her dress was very different from the Spanish,
Simpler, and yet of colors not so grave;
    For, as you know, the Spanish women banish
Bright hues when out of doors, and yet, while wave
    Around them (what I hope will never vanish)
The basquina and the mantilla, they
    Seem at the same time mystical and gay.

But with our damsel this was not the case:
    Her dress was many-color'd, finely spun;
Her locks curl'd negligently round her face,
    But through them gold and gems profusely shone;
Her girdle sparkled, and the richest lace
    Flow'd in her veil, and many a precious stone
Flash'd on her little hand; but, what was shocking,
Her small snow feet had slippers, but no stocking.

And Haidée met the morning face to face;
    Her own was freshest, though a feverish flush
Had dyed it with the headlong blood, whose race
    From heart to cheek is curb'd into a blush.

Like to a torrent which a mountain's base,
  That overpowers some Alpine river's rush,
Checks to a lake, whose waves in circles spread;
  Or the Red Sea—but the sea is not red.

And down the cliff the island virgin came,
  And near the cave her quick light footsteps drew,
While the sun smiled on her with his first flame,
  And young Aurora kiss'd her lips with dew,
Taking her for a sister; just the same
  Mistake you would have made on seeing the two,
Although the mortal, quite as fresh and fair,
Had all the advantage, too, of not being air.

And when into the cavern Haidée stepp'd
  All timidly, yet rapidly, she saw
That like an infant Juan sweetly slept;
  And then she stopp'd, and stood as if in awe,
(For sleep is awful,) and on tiptoe crept
  And wrapp'd him closer, lest the air, too raw,
Should reach his blood, then o'er him still as death
Bent, with hush'd lips, that drank his scarce-drawn breath.

He woke and gazed, and would have slept again,
  But the fair face which met his eyes forbade
Those eyes to close, though weariness and pain
  Had further sleep a further pleasure made;
For woman's face was never form'd in vain
  For Juan, so that even when he pray'd
He turn'd from grisly saints, and martyrs hairy,
To the sweet portraits of the Virgin Mary.

And thus upon his elbow he arose,
  And look'd upon the lady, in whose cheek
The pale contended with the purple rose,
  As with an effort she began to speak;
Her eyes were eloquent, her words would pose,
  Although she told him, in good modern Greek,
With an Ionian accent, low and sweet,
That he was faint, and must not talk, but eat.

Now Juan could not understand a word,
  Being no Grecian; but he had an ear,
And her voice was the warble of a bird,
  So soft, so sweet, so delicately clear,
That finer, simpler music, ne'er was heard;
  The sort of sound we echo with a tear,
Without knowing why—an overpowering tone,
Whence Melody descends as from a throne.

*   *   *   *   *

Of all the dresses I select Haidée's:
  She wore two jelicks—one was of pale yellow;
Of azure, pink, and white was her chemise—
  'Neath which her breast heaved like a little billow;
With buttons form'd of pearls as large as peas,
  All gold and crimson shone her jelick's fellow,
And the striped white gauze baracan that bound her,
Like fleecy clouds about the moon, flow'd round her.

One large gold bracelet clasp'd each lovely arm,
  Lockless—so pliable from the pure gold,
That the hand stretch'd and shut it without harm,
  The limb which it adorn'd its only mould;

So beautiful—its very shape would charm,
    And clinging as if loath to lose its hold,
The purest ore enclosed the whitest skin
    That e'er by precious metal was held in.

Around, as princess of her father's land,
    A like gold bar above her instep roll'd,
Announced her rank; twelve rings were on her hand;
    Her hair was starr'd with gems; her veil's fine fold
Below her breast was fasten'd with a band
    Of lavish pearls, whose worth could scarce be told;
Her orange silk full Turkish trousers furl'd
Above the prettiest ankle in the world.

Her hair's long auburn waves down to her heel
    Flow'd like an Alpine torrent which the sun
Dyes with his morning light,—and would conceal
    Her person if allow'd at large to run,
And still they seem resentfully to feel
    The silken fillet's curb, and sought to shun
Their bonds whene'er some Zephyr caught began
To offer his young pinion as her fan.

Round her she made an atmosphere of life,
    The very air seem'd lighter from her eyes,
They were so soft and beautiful, and rife
    With all we can imagine of the skies,
And pure as Psyche ere she grew a wife—
    Too pure even for the purest human ties;
Her overpowering presence made you feel
It would not be idolatry to kneel.

Her eyelashes, though dark as night, were tinged,
   (It is the country's custom,) but in vain;
For those large black eyes were so blackly fringed,
   The glossy rebels mock'd the jetty stain,
And in their native beauty stood avenged:
   Her nails were touch'd with henna; but again
The power of art was turn'd to nothing, for
They could not look more rosy than before.

The henna should be deeply dyed to make
   The skin relieved appear more fairly fair;
She had no need of this, day ne'er will break
   On mountain tops more heavenly white than her;
The eye might doubt if it were well awake,
   She was so like a vision; I might err,
But Shakspeare also says, 'tis very silly
"To gild refined gold, or paint the lily."

ZOE.

The other female's dress was not unlike,
    But of inferior materials: she
Had not so many ornaments to strike,
    Her hair had silver only, bound to be
Her dowry; and her veil, in form alike,
    Was coarser; and her air, though firm, less free;
Her hair was thicker, but less long; her eyes
As black, but quicker, and of smaller size.

She knew that the best feelings must have victual,
    And that a shipwreck'd youth would hungry be;
Besides, being less in love, she yawn'd a little,
    And felt her veins chill'd by the neighboring sea;
And so, she cook'd their breakfast to a tittle;
    I can't say that she gave them any tea,
But there were eggs, fruit, coffee, bread, fish, honey,
With Scio wine,—and all for love, not money.

And Zoe, when the eggs were ready, and
  The coffee made, would fain have waken'd Juan;
But Haidée stopp'd her with her quick small hand,
  And without word, a sign her finger drew on
Her lip, which Zoe needs must understand;
  And the first breakfast spoil'd, prepared a new one,
Because her mistress would not let her break
That sleep which seem'd as it would ne'er awake.

GULBEYAZ.

Her presence was as lofty as her state;
  Her beauty of that overpowering kind,
Whose force description only would abate:
  I'd rather leave it much to your own mind,
Than lessen it by what I could relate
  Of forms and features; it would strike you blind
Could I do justice to the full detail;
So, luckily for both, my phrases fail.

She spake some words to her attendants, who
  Composed a choir of girls, ten or a dozen,
And were all clad alike; like Juan, too,
  Who wore their uniform, by Baba chosen;
They form'd a very nymph-like looking crew,
  Which might have call'd Diana's chorus "cousin,"
As far as outward show may correspond;
I won't be bail for any thing beyond.

They bow'd obeisance and withdrew, retiring,
   But not by the same door through which came in
Baba and Juan, which last stood admiring,
   At some small distance, all he saw within
This strange saloon, much fitted for inspiring
   Marvel and praise; for both or none things win;
And I must say, I ne'er could see the very
Great happiness of the "Nil Admirari."

Baba, when all the damsels were withdrawn,
   Motion'd to Juan to approach, and then
A second time desired him to kneel down,
   And kiss the lady's foot; which maxim when
He heard repeated, Juan with a frown
   Drew himself up to his full height again,
And said, "It grieved him, but he could not stoop
To any shoe, unless it shod the Pope."

Baba, indignant at this ill-timed pride,
   Made fierce remonstrances, and then a threat
He mutter'd (but the last was given aside)
   About a bow-string—quite in vain; not yet
Would Juan bend, though 'twere to Mahomet's bride:
   There's nothing in the world like *etiquette*
In kingly chambers or imperial halls,
As also at the race and county balls.

He stood like Atlas, with a world of words
   About his ears, and nathless would not bend;
The blood of all his line's Castilian lords
   Boil'd in his veins, and rather than descend

To stain his pedigree a thousand swords
    A thousand times of him had made an end;
At length perceiving the "*foot*" could not stand,
Baba proposed that he should kiss the hand.

Here was an honorable compromise,
    A half-way house of diplomatic rest,
Where they might meet in much more peaceful guise;
    And Juan now his willingness express'd,
To use all fit and proper courtesies,
    Adding, that this was commonest and best,
For through the South the custom still commands
The gentleman to kiss the lady's hands.

The lady eyed him o'er and o'er, and bade
    Baba retire, which he obey'd in style,
As if well used to the retreating trade;
    And taking hints in good part all the while,
He whisper'd Juan not to be afraid,
    And looking on him with a sort of smile,
Took leave, with such a face of satisfaction,
As good men wear who have done a virtuous action.

When he was gone, there was a sudden change
    I know not what might be the lady's thought,
But o'er her bright brow flash'd a tumult strange,
    And into her clear cheek the blood was brought,
Blood-red as sunset summer clouds which range
    The verge of Heaven; and in her large eyes wrought,
A mixture of sensations might be scann'd,
Of half voluptuousness and half command.

Her very smile was haughty, though so sweet;
    Her very nod was not an inclination;
There was a self-will even in her small feet,
    As though they were quite conscious of her station—
They trod as upon necks; and to complete
    Her state, (it is the custom of her nation,)
A poniard deck'd her girdle, as the sign
She was a sultan's bride, (thank Heaven, not mine!)

To hear and to obey" had been from birth
    The law of all around her; to fulfil
All fantasies which yielded joy or mirth,
    Had been her slaves' chief pleasure, as her will;
Her blood was high, her beauty scarce of earth:
    Judge, then, if her caprices e'er stood still;
Had she but been a Christian, I've a notion
We should have found out the "perpetual motion."

Whate'er she saw and coveted was brought;
    Whate'er she did *not* see, if she supposed
It might be seen, with diligence was sought,
    And when 'twas found straightway the bargain closed:
There was no end unto the things she bought,
    Nor to the trouble which her fancies caused;
Yet even her tyranny had such a grace,
The women pardon'd all except her face.

KATINKA.

And yet they had their little jealousies,
    Like all the rest; but upon this occasion,
Whether there are such things as sympathies
    Without our knowledge or our approbation,
Although they could not see through his disguise,
    All felt a soft kind of concatenation,
Like magnetism, or devilism, or what
You please—we will not quarrel about that:

But certain 'tis they all felt for their new
    Companion something newer still, as 'twere
A sentimental friendship through and through,
    Extremely pure, which made them all concur
In wishing her their sister, save a few
    Who wish'd they had a brother just like her,
Whom, if they were at home in sweet Circassia,
They would prefer to Padisha or Pacha.

Of those who had most genius for this sort
   Of sentimental friendship, there were three,
Lolah, Katinka, and Dudù; in short,
   (To save description,) fair as fair can be
Were they, according to the best report,
   Though differing in stature and degree,
And clime and time, and country and complexion;
They all alike admired their new connection.

Lolah was dusk as India and as warm;
   Katinka was a Georgian, white and red,
With great blue eyes, a lovely hand and arm,
   And feet so small they scarce seem'd made to tread,
But rather skim the earth.

DUDÙ.

A KIND of sleepy Venus seem'd Dudù,
    Yet very fit to "murder sleep," in those
Who gazed upon her cheek's transcendent hue,
    Her Attic forehead, and her Phidian nose:
Few angles were there in her form, 'tis true,
    Thinner she might have been, and yet scarce lose;
Yet, after all, 'twould puzzle to say where
It would not spoil some separate charm to *pare*.

She was not violently lively, but
    Stole on your spirit like a May-day breaking;
Her eyes were not too sparkling, yet, half-shut,
    They put beholders in a tender taking;
She look'd (this simile's quite new) just cut
    From marble, like Pygmalion's statue waking,
The mortal and the marble still at strife,
And timidly expanding into life.

Dudù said nothing, but sat down beside
    Juanna, playing with her veil or hair;
And looking at her steadfastly, she sigh'd,
    As if she pitied her for being there,

A pretty stranger without friend or guide,
    And all abash'd, too, at the general stare
Which welcomes hapless strangers in all places,
With kind remarks upon their mien and faces.

Dudù, as has been said, was a sweet creature,
    Not very dashing, but extremely winning,
With the most regulated charms of feature,
    Which painters cannot catch like faces sinning
Against proportion—the wild strokes of nature
    Which they hit off at once in the beginning,
Full of expression, right or wrong, that strike,
And pleasing, or unpleasing, still are like.

But she was a soft landscape of mild earth,
    Where all was harmony, and calm, and quiet,
Luxuriant, budding; cheerful without mirth,
    Which, if not happiness, is much more nigh it
Than are your mighty passions and so forth,
    Which some call "the sublime:" I wish they'd try it:
I've seen your stormy seas and stormy women;
And pity lovers rather more than seamen.

But she was pensive more than melancholy,
    And serious more than pensive, and serene,
It may be, more than either—not unholy
    Her thoughts, at least till now, appear to have been.
The strangest thing was, beauteous, she was wholly
    Unconscious, albeit turn'd of quick seventeen,
That she was fair, or dark, or short, or tall;
She never thought about herself at all.

LADY PINCHBECK.

But first of little Leila we'll dispose;
   For like a day-dawn she was young and pure,
Or like the old comparison of snows,
   Which are more pure than pleasant to be sure.
Like many people everybody knows,
   Don Juan was delighted to secure
A goodly guardian for his infant charge,
Who might not profit much by being at large.

Besides, he had found out he was no tutor,
   (I wish that others would find out the same;)
And rather wish'd in such things to stand neuter,
   For silly wards will bring their guardians blame:
So when he saw each ancient dame a suitor
   To make his little wild Asiatic tame,
Consulting "the Society for Vice
Suppression," Lady Pinchbeck was his choice.

Olden she was—but had been very young;
    Virtuous she was—and had been, I believe;
Although the world has such an evil tongue
    That——but my chaster ear will not receive
An echo of a syllable that's wrong:
    In fact, there's nothing makes me so much grieve,
As that abominable tittle-tattle,
Which is the cud eschew'd by human cattle.

I said that Lady Pinchbeck had been talked about—
    As who has not, if female, young, and pretty?
But now no more the ghost of Scandal stalk'd about;
    She merely was deem'd amiable and witty,
And several of her best bon-mots were hawk'd about:
    Then she was given to charity and pity,
And pass'd (at least the latter years of life)
For being a most exemplary wife.

High in high circles, gentle in her own,
    She was the mild reprover of the young,
Whenever—which means every day—they'd shown
    An awkward inclination to go wrong.
The quantity of good she did 's unknown,
    Or at the least would lengthen out my song:
In brief, the little orphan of the East
Had raised an interest in her, which increased.

AURORA RABY.

And then there was—but why should I go on,
    Unless the ladies should go off?—there was
Indeed a certain fair and fairy one,
    Of the best class, and better than her class,—
Aurora Raby, a young star who shone
    O'er life, too sweet an image for such glass,
A lovely being, scarcely form'd or moulded,
A rose with all its sweetest leaves yet folded;

Rich, noble, but an orphan; left an only
    Child to the care of guardians good and kind;
But still her aspect had an air so lonely!
    Blood is not water; and where shall we find
Feelings of youth like those which overthrown lie
    By death, when we are left, alas! behind,
To feel, in friendless palaces, a home
Is wanting, and our best ties in the tomb?

Early in years, and yet more infantine
   In figure, she had something of sublime
In her eyes which sadly shone, as seraphs' shine.
   All youth—but with an aspect beyond time;
Radiant and grave—as pitying man's decline;
   Mournful—but mornful of another's crime,
She look'd as if she sat by Eden's door,
And grieved for those who could return no more.

She was a Catholic, too, sincere, austere,
   As far as her own gentle heart allow'd,
And deem'd that fallen worship far more dear
   Perhaps because 'twas fallen: her sires were proud
Of deeds and days when they had fill'd the ear
   Of nations, and had never bent or bow'd
To novel power; and as she was the last,
She held their old faith and old feelings fast.

She gazed upon a world she scarcely knew
   As seeking not to know it; silent, lone,
As grows a flower, thus quietly she grew,
   And kept her heart serene within its zone.
There was awe in the homage which she drew;
   Her spirit seem'd as seated on a throne
Apart from the surrounding world, and strong
In its own strength—most strange in one so young!

Now it so happen'd, in the catalogue
   Of Adeline, Aurora was omitted,
Although her birth and wealth had given her vogue,
   Beyond the charmers we have already cited:

Her beauty also seem'd to form no clog
  Against her being mention'd as well fitted,
By many virtues, to be worth the trouble
Of single gentlemen who would be double.

And this omission, like that of the bust
  Of Brutus at the pageant of Tiberius,
Made Juan wonder, as no doubt he must.
  This he express'd half smiling and half serious;
When Adeline replied with some disgust,
  And with an air, to say the least, imperious,
She marvell'd " what he saw in such a baby
As that prim, silent, cold Aurora Raby?"

Little Aurora deem'd she was the theme
  Of such discussion. She was there a guest;
A beauteous ripple of the brilliant stream
  Of rank and youth, though purer than the rest,
Which flow'd on for a moment in the beam
  Time sheds a moment o'er each sparkling crest.
Had she known this, she would have calmly smiled—
She had so much, or little, of the child.

The dashing and proud air of Adeline
  Imposed not upon her: she saw her blaze
Much as she would have seen a glow-worm shine,
  Then turn'd unto the stars for loftier rays.
Juan was something she could not divine,
  Being no sibyl in the new world's ways;
Yet she was nothing dazzled by the meteor,
Because she did not pin her faith on feature.

His fame too,—for he had that kind of fame,
    Which sometimes plays the deuce with womankind,
A heterogeneous mass of glorious blame,
    Half virtues and whole vices being combined;
Faults which attract because they are not tame;
    Follies trick'd out so brightly that they blind:—
These seals upon her wax made no impression,
Such was her coldness or her self-possession.

Juan knew naught of such a character—
    High, yet resembling not his lost Haidée;
Yet each was radiant in her proper sphere:
    The island girl, bred up by the lone sea,
More warm, as lovely, and not less sincere,
    Was Nature's all: Aurora could not be,
Nor would be thus:—the difference in them
Was such as lies between a flower and gem.

DUCHESS OF FITZ-FULKE.

She was a fine and somewhat full-blown blonde,
   Desirable, distinguish'd, celebrated
For several winters in the grand, *grand monde*.
   I'd rather not say what might be related
Of her exploits, for this were ticklish ground;
   Besides, there might be falsehood in what's stated.
Her late performance had been a dead set
At Lord Augustus Fitz-Plantagenet.

This noble personage began to look
   A little black upon this new flirtation;
But such small licenses must lovers brook,
   Mere freedoms of the female corporation.
Wo to the man who ventures a rebuke!
   'Twill but precipitate a situation
Extremely disagreeable, but common
To calculators when they count on woman.

The circle smiled, then whisper'd, and then sneer'd;
   The Misses bridled, and the matrons frown'd;
Some hoped things might not turn out as they fear'd;
   Some would not deem such women could be found;
Some ne'er believed one half of what they heard;
   Some look'd perplex'd, and others look'd profound:
And several pitied with sincere regret
Poor Lord Augustus Fitz-Plantagenet.

But what is odd, none ever named the duke,
   Who, one might think, was something in the affair:
True, he was absent, and, 'twas rumor'd, took
   But small concern about the when, or where,
Or what his consort did: if he could brook
   Her gayeties, none had a right to stare:
Theirs was that best of unions, past all doubt,
Which ever meets, and therefore can't fall out.

  * * * * * *

    —— Lo! a monk, array'd
   In cowl and beads, and dusky garb, appear'd,
Now in the moonlight, and now lapsed in shade,
   With steps that trod as heavy, yet unheard;
His garments only a slight murmur made;
   He moved as shadowy as the sisters weird,
But slowly; and as he pass'd Juan by,
Glanced, without pausing, on him a bright eye.

Juan was petrified; he had heard a hint
    Of such a spirit in these halls of old,
But thought, like most men, there was nothing in 't
    Beyond the rumor which such spots unfold,
Coin'd from surviving superstition's mint,
    Which passes ghosts in currency like gold,
But rarely seen, like gold compared with paper,
And did he see this? or was it a vapor?

Once, twice, thrice pass'd, repass'd—the thing of air,
    Or earth beneath, or heaven, or t' other place:
And Juan gazed upon it with a stare,
    Yet could not speak or move; but, on its base
As stands a statue, stood: he felt his hair
    Twine like a knot of snakes around his face;
He tax'd his tongue for words, which were not granted,
To ask the reverend person what he wanted.

The third time, after a still longer pause,
    The shadow pass'd away—but where? the hall
Was long, and thus far there was no great cause
    To think his vanishing unnatural:
Doors there were many, through which, by the laws
    Of physics, bodies whether short or tall
Might come or go; but Juan could not state
Through which the spectre seem'd to evaporate.

He stood—how long, he knew not, but it seem'd
    An age—expectant, powerless, with his eyes
Strain'd on the spot where first the figure gleam'd;
    Then by degrees recalled his energies,

And would have pass'd the whole off as a dream,
   But could not wake; he was, he did surmise,
'Waking already, and return'd at length
Back to his chamber, shorn of half his strength.

  *   *   *   *   *

The door flew wide, not swiftly,—but, as fly
   The sea-gulls, with a steady, sober flight—
And then swung back; nor close—but stood awry,
   Half letting in long shadows on the light,
Which still in Juan's candlesticks burn'd high,
   For he had two, both tolerably bright,
And in the door-way, darkening darkness, stood
The sable friar in his solemn hood.

Don Juan shook, as erst he had been shaken
   The night before; but being sick of shaking,
He first inclined to think he had been mistaken;
   And then to be ashamed of such mistaking;
His own internal ghost began to awaken
   Within him, and to quell his corporal quaking—
Hinting that soul and body on the whole
Were odds against a disembodied soul.

And then his dread grew wrath, and his wrath fierce,
   And he arose, advanced—the shade retreated:
But Juan, eager now the truth to pierce,
   Follow'd, his veins no longer cold, but heated,
Resolved to trust the mystery carte and tierce,
   At whatsoever risk of being defeated:

The ghost stopp'd, menaced, then retired, until
He reach'd the ancient wall, then stood stone still.

Juan put forth one arm—Eternal powers!
　It touch'd no soul, no body, but the wall,
On which the moonbeams fell in silvery showers,
　Checker'd with all the tracery of the hall;
He shudder'd, as no doubt the bravest cowers
　When he can't tell what 'tis that doth appal.
How odd, a single hobgoblin's nonentity
Should cause more fear than a whole host's identity.

But still the shade remain'd: the blue eyes glared,
　And rather variably for stony death;
Yet one thing rather good the grave had spared,
　The ghost had a remarkably sweet breath:
A straggling curl show'd he had been fair-hair'd;
　A red lip, with two rows of pearls beneath,
Gleam'd forth, as through the casement's ivy shroud
The moon peep'd, just escaped from a gray cloud.

And Juan, puzzled, but still curious, thrust
　His other arm forth—Wonder upon wonder!
It press'd upon a hard but glowing bust,
　Which beat as if there was a warm heart under.
He found, as people on most trials must,
　That he had made at first a silly blunder,
And that in his confusion he had caught
Only the wall, instead of what he sought.

The ghost, if ghost it were, seem'd a sweet soul
    As ever lurk'd beneath a holy hood :
A dimpled chin, a neck of ivory, stole
    Forth into something much like flesh and blood ;
Back fell the sable frock and dreary cowl,
    And they reveal'd—alas! that e'er they should!
In full, voluptuous, but *not o'er*grown bulk,
The phantom of her frolic Grace—Fitz-Fulke!

THE END.

www.ingramcontent.com/pod-product-compliance
Lightning Source LLC
Chambersburg PA
CBHW032205230426
43672CB00011B/2511